Critical Guides to Spanish Texts

Critical Guides to Spanish Texts

EDITED BY J.E. VAREY, A.D. DEYERMOND, AND S.M. HART

54 Pérez Galdós: Nazarín

Critical Guides to Spanish Texts

EDITED BY J.E. VAREY, A.D. DEYERMOND, AND S.M. HART

PEREZ GALDOS

Nazarín

Peter Bly

Professor of Spanish,
Queen's University, Kingston, Ontario

Grant & Cutler Ltd *in association with*
Tamesis Books Ltd 1991

© Grant & Cutler Ltd 1991

ISBN 0 7293 0329 2

60 036 00787

I.S.B.N. 84-599-3253-2

DEPÓSITO LEGAL: V. 2.843 - 1991

Printed in Spain by
Artes Gráficas Soler, S.A., Valencia
for
GRANT & CUTLER LTD
55-57 GREAT MARLBOROUGH STREET, LONDON W1V 2AY

Contents

For Declan

Preface

References to the text of *Nazarín* are from the most recent edition (Madrid: Alianza, 1984), pp.210; they indicate the Part and Chapter numbers followed by the page number, thus: II, v; 63. References to other works by Galdós are taken from the *Obras completas*, ed. F. C. Sainz de Robles, 6 vols (Madrid: Aguilar, 1961-69), indicated thus: OC, VI, 1050, unless otherwise stated.

The figures in parentheses in italic type refer to the numbered items in the Bibliographical Note; where necessary these are followed by page numbers, thus: *5*, p.112.

An invited paper, *'Nazarín* as a Series of Interviews', given to the Modern Novel class of Dr Victor Ouimette, McGill University, in 1985 contained an embryonic version of some comments to be found in Chapters 1 and 2b of this study.

I should like to acknowledge the generous assistance of the Social Sciences and Humanities Research Council of Canada: a research grant allowed me to gather material in Madrid as well as to prepare the text of this study. I am also very grateful to Professors J. E. Varey and A. D. Deyermond, the editors of this series, for their kind and helpful comments on the draft of this book. Finally, I should like to thank Mrs Paulette Bark for her careful and swift typing of the text, and also my parents, wife and children for their patience and understanding at all times during its preparation.

Peter Bly
Kingston, Ontario
July 1987

Abbreviations

AG   *Anales Galdosianos*
CHA   *Cuadernos Hispanoamericanos*
EM   *La España Moderna*
In   *Insula*

1 Galdós's Prologue: Part I as Lesson in Reading Strategies

The Title and Nomenclature

The reader of *Nazarín* is confronted with a verbal problem before he turns the title page (5, p.112): what does the word 'Nazarín' mean? Is it an adjective or noun? Does it refer to a person or thing? Its form suggests some possible relation to 'nazareno', a word with multiple meanings: a Nazarite (a member of a religious sect which forbade alcohol consumption and hair-cutting); a native of Nazareth; Christ; his follower/iconographical representation; or participant in Holy Week celebrations. Another possible source, enlarging the Judeo-Christian connotations of 'nazareno' (*15*) to include the third of Spain's major religious groups in the Middle Ages, the Arabs, is the word 'Nazarí', a follower or descendant of Yúsuf ben Názar, a thirteenth-century ruler of Granada. Finally, what meaning (diminutiveness or affection) is to be given to the suffix '-ín'? The reader, though perhaps only partially aware of these connotations, realizes that he is about to read a novel whose text might also prove difficult to interpret. Indeed, the opening sentence - the longest in all of Galdós's novels (7, p.81) - forwards the process of mystification by its involved syntactical structure. The subject of the main verb "debo" is the narrator, who wants to establish his debt to a journalist for discovering the boarding house of a 'la tía *Chanfaina*'. It is ironic that the main point is not the establishment of an omniscient narrator's authority but the admission of his dependence on other actors in the fiction. Moreover, the significance of this admission is concealed somewhat by the arrangement of more extensive word groupings at the beginning and end of the sentence. The first outlines

the various news items covered by the journalist, the second refers to
the street in which *Chanfaina's* establishment is located. What,
precisely, is the main point the narrator wishes to make, or are all
three equally significant?

On the other hand, the narrator seems remarkably aware of the
need to find the right word to express the reality reproduced:
'designamos' is the first verb in the sentence. He substitutes the
currently fashionable foreign import 'repórter' (suitably italicized) to
describe more accurately the journalists 'de nuevo cuño' (I, i; 9). He
authoritatively informs us that on her baptismal certificate,
Chanfaina's name was entered as Estefanía, but without explaining
the relation of the two forms or, indeed, their contrasted meanings,
'cheap stew' and 'crown', respectively. The third example of the
narrator's linguistic competence is perhaps the most important:
having shown that new realities need new words, that one person or
object can have more than one designation, he now points out how
words can misrepresent, not correspond to, reality: the 'mezquinidad
y pobreza' of the street in which *Chanfaina's* 'casa de huéspedes' is
located, 'contrastan del modo más irónico con su altísono y corus-
cante nombre: *calle de las Amazonas*' (I, i; 9). And yet, in retrospect,
given the size of *Chanfaina's* body and the scenes of physical
violence that will occur in the boarding house (including some of
those listed as news items for the reporter — fires, fights, suicides —
and belittled by the narrator's metaphor of the greyhound chasing the
hare), the street name will appear far from inappropriate or ironic.

What is ironic is the contrast between the narrator's inability to
perceive the significance of some of his own remarks and his
extreme sensitivity to the deceit of language at other times. In calling
attention — unwittingly — to his own limitations as a narrator, he
not only presents himself as a mirror figure (*32*, p.66) for the reader
as he stumbles from insight to obscurity on a first reading, but also
establishes — again unwittingly — the potentially obfuscatory
nature of a text that is supposed to be an 'historia' (I, i; 10).

The narrator now makes an important association between this
onomastic discrepancy and a seemingly much larger but undefined
process of deception: it is part and parcel of 'la eterna *guasa* de

Madrid' or 'la ciudad (o villa) del sarcasmo y las mentiras maleantes' (I, i; 9). The narrator quickly identifies himself as a member of that group who can see through such farce (linguistic or otherwise) by providing for the less privileged a pompously erudite account of the etymology of the street's name. Yet the narrator's pride as a 'sagaz cronista' filling in this gap ('*vacío*') is punctured by a number of devices: his introductory familiar language ('qué amazonas fueron esas que la bautizaron, ni de dónde vinieron, ni qué demonios se les había perdido en los Madroñales del Oso' (yet another, appropriately sylvan, epithet for Madrid)'; his inability to relate this 'festejo' or 'divertimiento' (I, i; 10), the celebration of Queen Isabel de Valois's entry into the capital in the sixteenth century by prostitutes dressed up as mounted 'heroínas mitológicas', to the previously established 'eterna guasa de Madrid', or to chronicle the exact date of the histori- cal event ('en tiempos de Mari-Castaña') or even to anticipate Nazarín's parallel entry at the end of the novel. Forming the climax of this deflationary process is the narrator's admission, echoing the verbal form and syntactic slyness of his first debt, that he owes these 'profundas sabidurías' to an 'ingenuo *avisador* coetáneo' (a historical forerunner of the contemporary reporter) (I, i; 10).[1] The narrator seems impervious to the effects that this or a subsequent admission that he does not know the correct designation for the Amazons might have on the reader's confidence in his authority.

   Our disconcerting narrator can now confidently declare that *Chanfaina* is directly descended from these Amazons, but he cannot,

---

[1]In actual fact, this quotation and some of the preceding narrative are taken verbatim from Galdós's contemporary, Antonio Capmani y Montpalau, *Origen histórico y etimológico de las calles de Madrid* (Madrid: Quirós, 1863), p.21. 'Debo' is repeated a third time in the third paragraph of this opening chapter when the narrator now acknowledges his debt to *Chanfaina*'s 'barbarie' for 'el germen de la presente historia'. There is a curious pattern of ironic interlocking verbal echoes in this opening chapter. The 'designamos' of the first paragraph is echoed by the 'designaba el vulgo' of the second, whereas *Chanfaina*'s 'fe de bautismo' reverberates in 'qué amazonas fueron esas que la bautizaron' in the first. Of course, such repetition could be suitably interpreted as a sign of the narrator's forgetfulness or weak style.

to his annoyance, get her name correct: two more forms (there could be even more) are now added to the two originally given: '*Estefanía la del Peñón, Chanfaina*, o como demonios se llame' (I, i; 10). He is even capable of certifying a linguistic non-event, 'digo con toda verdad que se me despega la pluma, cuando quiero aplicárselo, el apacible nombre de mujer' (I, i; 10), or of prophesying future events: *Chanfaina* is the most formidable 'tarasca, que vieron los antiguos Madriles [the fifth designation of the capital in two pages] y esperan ver los venideros' (I, i; 10).

The narrator's flitting from one subject to another in quick succession reappears in paragraph three when having mentioned his friend, the reporter, *Chanfaina* and — for the first time — Nazarín (though not by name, just as the 'singularísimo personaje que le da nombre [a la historia]'), he suddenly launches into a dense description of the boarding house, which had seemed the centre of his attention in the novel's opening sentence. Yet his sudden warning that 'No tome nadie al pie de la letra lo de *casa de huéspedes* que al principio se ha dicho' (I, i: 10) instantly confirms the readers' growing suspicions about the narrator's authority: he no longer confuses with single words or phrases, but — far more seriously — wittingly and wilfully manipulates the sequence of words and ideas. Consequently, it is not surprising that, as well as being unaware of the serious implications of his admission — it immediately makes all of Part I, if not the whole novel (*32*, p.59), liable to similar revisions by the reader — the narrator contradicts himself, for he says next that the only similarity between *Chanfaina*'s establishment and those in central Madrid is 'la del nombre' (I, i; 10-11), a name we have been asked not to take at face value, as perhaps we no longer do with the other 'nombres' previously mentioned: *repórter*, the street name and that of the novel. The reason for this discrepancy of meaning behind single words is clear for all to see in the narrator's personal and misguided assumption that all of his readers have known central Madrid boarding houses in their student or later days (even if the narrator himself does not see it). Each individual may use the same word, but the precise meaning attached to it will vary according to personal experience or lack of it.

Having thus alerted the reader, through the narrator's mixture
of perceptiveness and obtuseness, on how to approach the text,
Galdós now turns to another illustration to repeat his point: an
emblematic picture of the building whose designation is apparently
such a misnomer.

Chanfaina's Boarding House

To emphasize the visual nature of this second lesson Galdós employs
pictorial terminology, with some justification, for although dirty and
dilapidated, the entrance has taken on an artistic appearance through
the constant peeling of the plaster: a mosaic of 'mil fantásticos
dibujos', with the bare bones of the wall exposed in a few places. In
short, the portal is a visual emblem of how to read Nazarín's story:
the whole will, despite its heterogeneous material, be a work of art,
capable of multiple and equally fantastic interpretations, with the
truth discernible only on odd occasions. The inner walls of the patio,
appropriately referred to by 'lienzo', a term which also has artistic
connotations, and dating from different epochs, also present an artistic fantasy, which is now more emphatically inserted into the
surrounding 'guasa de Madrid'. The structures of the patio are a
'broma arquitectónica':

> ventanas que querían bajar, puertas que se estiraban para
> subir, barandillas convertidas en tabiques, paredes
> rezumadas por la humedad, canalones oxidados y
> torcidos, tejas en los alféizares, planchas de cinc
> claveteadas sobre podridas maderas para cerrar un
> hueco, ángulos chafados[...] caballetes erizados de
> vidrios y cascos de botella para amedrentar a la ratería;
> por un lado, pies derechos carcomidos sustentando una
> galería que se inclina como un barco varado; por otro,
> puertas de cuarterones con gateras tan grandes que por
> ellas cabrían tigres si allí los hubiese; rejas de color de
> canela; trozos de ladrillo amoratado, como coágulos de
> sangre; y, por fin, los escarceos de la luz y la sombra en

todos aquellos ángulos cortantes y oquedades siniestras.
(I, i; 11)

The normal shapes and lines of architectural components have become comically distorted, converted, or covered by other materials, for a different purpose. If one 'hueco' in the wood is blocked up by a zinc plate (and we recall the narrator filling in a 'vacío' in the history of the street name with his erudition), then others are left gaping, big enough for tigers to jump through. The qualifying phrase 'si allí los hubiese' is not so fanciful as at first sight appears, for whilst it reinforces the 'fiera' designation of *Chanfaina* and the name of the street, some of its occupants will soon act like wild animals and blood will be spilt, as if to confirm the description of pieces of red brick as clots of blood. The mention of broken glass atop walls to repel robbers is another feature that refers back to the narrator's opening remarks on the sensational news items covered by the reporter as well as anticipating future events.

The narrator now adds some chronological precision to his narrative, yet, not surprisingly, he is somewhat less than totally informative: the visit to *Chanfaina*'s establishment takes place on the most appropriate day in the calendar, a Martes de Carnaval, but the year is not given, leaving open a whole range of possibilities in the recent or immediate past. The nature of this visit, with such important consequences for the novel, is then clarified to a certain extent: it is not a pre-arranged expedition by the two men, but rather a chance meeting outside the entrance, again appropriate for a Shrove Tuesday: 'tuvo el buen reportero la humorada de dar conmigo en aquellos sitios' (I, i; 11).

The characters they meet in the patio are a varied group whose dress and appearance are described in perhaps more precise detail than their status as non-reappearing extras would warrant. Yet the identity of these types and their activities are not without significance for the ambience of enigma and ambiguity that Galdós is constantly seeking to establish through his narrator in Part I: the lady who sells liquid refreshments at the entrance is a 'tuerta', whilst some gypsies are tending their donkeys (one old man's whiskers are the same texture as the coat of the animal he is combing). On the one day in the year's calendar when everybody is concealing their normal identity, the narrator hardly needs to say more about the gypsies' notorious reputation for disguising the true identity and health of horses and donkeys. But after their chance encounter, it is perhaps appropriate that the two men be reminded of the role of chance in human affairs by the gypsies' offer to practise another of their traditional skills: fortunetelling.

Contrasts are also visible between the trade of the 'mieleros' and their thin, cooked-meat appearance, or between the destitute appearance of the trio of buskers and their imbibing of brandy before they start begging in the streets. But by far the most important deceivers the two men meet as they make their way inside the building, as to be expected on Shrove Tuesday, are 'las máscaras', the single word denoting a variety of types: transvestites, coloured faces, grotesque face masks (of such a leader of normal society as the Prime Minister), theatrical costumes, paper hats and dress mantillas. In order to point up the absurdly empty disguise of this assortment of 'máscaras', two characters with a real facial mask — that of death or near-death — are wheeled out of the patio: a female centenarian, used as a decoy for alms, and whose face is like an enlarged chestnut, would have appeared like a mummy 'si sus ojuelos claros no revelaran un resto de vida en aquel lío de huesos y piel, olvidado por la muerte' (I, i; 13). Death has remembered to take a two-year old boy whose corpse is now carried out, but not before his father has taken his glass of brandy. The reverse of the pretence and playfulness of Shrove Tuesday is the reminder of the Death of Ash Wednesday: 'las máscaras' of disguise are confronted with the true masks of death or near-death. The narrator again confounds us with his sudden inclusion of such a discordant but noteworthy detail and in language of considerable feeling and force, seldom equalled in the rest of Galdós's work: the corpse of the child 'Salió sin aparato de lágrimas ni despedida maternal, como si nadie existiera en el mundo que con pena le viera salir[...] sólo las gitanas tuvieron una palabra de lástima para aquel ser que tan de prisa pasaba por nuestro mundo' (I, i; 13).[2]

There is movement in and out of this 'extraña mansión' (I, i; 14) temporarily and permanently, both in the present and the past (*Chanfaina*'s former, more affluent, clients have moved into the city centre). These continual movements forming the 'estructuras dinámicas' of the novel (7, p.81) remind us that nothing in this novel can be eternally fixed, stable or definitive: there can only be movement, change and perplexity.

Chanfaina

The landlady's body presents a disturbing mixture of contrasting features: her hair is well combed 'con sinfín de garabatos, ondas y sortijillas' (I, ii; 14) but the rest of her appearance is dishevelled. Her voluminous stomach and chest, her wide neck and bullish nose contrast with the traces of 'una belleza de brocha gorda, abultada, barroca' in her face. Furthermore, it is difficult to put these features into proper optical focus: *Chanfaina* is like 'una ninfa de pintura de techos, dibujada para ser vista de lejos, y que se ve de cerca' (I, i-ii; 14).

The amazon's speech also disorients the readers. Here she shows good verbal skills in painting her own character; they are so good, in fact, that the portrait could well be a distortion, as the narrator unwittingly intimates: 'Hizo, en fin, la descripción de su carácter con una sinceridad que parecía de ley, no fingida' (I, ii; 15). Indeed, she may like to see herself as a kind-hearted, debt-forgiving

---

[2]For Galdós's own largely negative views on Carnaval see *Los artículos de Galdós en La Nación (1865-1866, 1868)*, ed. W.H. Shoemaker (Madrid: Insula, 1972), pp.37-39, 275-78, 412, 435; *Las cartas desconocidas de Galdós en 'La Prensa' de Buenos Aires*, ed. William H. Shoemaker (Madrid: Cultura Hispánica, 1973), pp.69-71, 223-25. The 23 February 1895 number of *La Ilustración Ibérica* reported that the 'máscaras' of Moors and gypsies were the most popular designs. Can we say, therefore, with total certainty that the gypsies the narrator saw in *Chanfaina*'s patio are not 'máscaras' or that Nazarín is not wearing a Moorish one (6, p.215)? In the last analysis, we only have the narrator's word to rely on.

mother-figure for her tenants, but she is also the madame of a brothel, as the intrusion of four resident prostitutes or 'tarascas' (originally meaning a Corpus Christi dragon figure) suddenly reveals. The narrator avoids such an explicit designation, and, indeed, in his typically confusing order of narration, leads the readers to believe at first that these are ordinary women carrying masks. But this impression is soon corrected, for 'el antifaz de cartón' is really facial paint. Finally, the cheap perfume and coarse speech of the women reveal their status as 'lo más abyecto y zarrapastroso de la especie humana' (I, ii; 15). The narrator would now have us believe that this process of unmasking took less time than it seems to have done, as if he does not want to appear so slow-witted: 'Al pronto, habría podido creerse que eran máscaras y el colorete una forma extravagante de disfraz carnavalesco. Tal fue mi primera impresión; pero no tardé en conocer que la pintura era en ellas por todos estilos *ordinaria*, o que vivían siempre en Carnestolendas' (I, ii; 15). As with the dead child, so now with these prostitutes the narrator notes a more serious dimension to life on this Shrove Tuesday but without commenting on it at length or with fuller understanding. He half perceives this dimension, just as he half hears the prostitutes' talk about a 'papel de alfileres y [...] un hombre'.

Nazarín

Could this man be Nazarín? The person whom the reporter and narrator then see framed by an open window first appears to be a woman. As with the four prostitutes, it is the voice that certifies his identity as a man. Nazarín's entry into the novel is suitably incorporated, then, into the gallery of visual and verbal enigmas hitherto presented. Other details strengthen his ambiguous appearance: his age (he could be middle-aged or prematurely old), his profession (he looks an Arab but is dressed as a Catholic priest), his dress (is it a 'sotana' or a 'balandrán'?), and his position in the boarding-house-cum-brothel: his window opens onto the patio but entry is not through an adjacent door (blocked up) but by a back staircase; his rooms are part of the building, yet they are not; he is not a paying lodger, yet he will now ask *Chanfaina* for food.

The reason he is obliged to do this is because his few possessions and food have been stolen. Nazarín's long complaint of this theft sounds discordant in a man who is said to be a priest. Besides slowly initiating the plot of the novel, Nazarín's tirade is also significant for linking him with the narrator through his obstinate self-assurance. If the latter can declare proudly, 'oímos un diálogo que mi excelente memoria me permite transcribir sin perder una sílaba' (only at the end to omit *Chanfaina*'s 'frases indecentes' 'por respeto a los que esto leyeren' (I, ii; 16, 17)), the priest, as if he were detailing the facts of the case for the reporter's paper, is most precise and certain: 'Pues que me han robado. No queda duda de que me han robado' (I, ii; 16); 'Ha sido la Siona. No hay que echar la culpa a nadie más que a la Siona' (I, ii; 18). Moreover, the plain language, sprinkled with a few colloquialisms, like 'señá *Chanfaina*' and 'esta es la más negra' (I, ii; 17) (to be repeated by the narrator at the start of the next chapter), will contrast with his rhetorical style of speech in the interview. *Chanfaina*'s retort, as well as illustrating her linguistic inventiveness, adds important modifications to Nazarín's unequivocal version of events: she wonders if the culprit was Siona, when he is constantly visited by people, for he is 'el espíritu de la confianza y de la bobería' (I, ii; 18), and he has lost things before. Moreoever, when Nazarín paces the room 'sin parecer muy afectado por sus desdichas' (I, ii; 17-18) and then suddenly drops the matter, the readers have to question his ability to put things into proper perspective: why, then, did he greet the two visitors with such a tirade on a matter that seems a trivial, daily occurrence? Like the narrator, Nazarín seems unaware of the implicit contradictions of his words and statements. The reporter now follows suit by declaring unabashedly that what will form the central question of the novel (is Nazarín a fool or a saint?) 'se ha de saber con toda certeza' (I, ii; 19) merely by talking to him. For a person who has met Nazarín before and immediately assumes that the priest's character and life history 'han de ser muy singulares, tan singulares como su tipo', the reporter possesses very little information about him, calling him paradoxically an 'árabe manchego', and is even uncertain about his correct name (no second surname is provided): don Nazario Zaharín o Zajarín (I, ii; 19). No explanation is given about the meaning or origins of the two names, whilst the reader deduces for himself that what had appeared on the title page to be a diminutive suffix, now represents a contraction of the surname.

The Interview

As if to undercut the reporter's sweeping assertion, the four prostitutes now reappear to hurl insults at Nazarín for accusing Siona of the theft. Their collective abuse suggests that the reporter's premises about Nazarín's character are out of focus, that indeed Nazarín is an irresponsible slanderer as well as being lazy. Their colourful language, besides filling in details about Nazarín's household and serving as a dynamic antidote to the anodyne clichés of the subsequent interview,[3] also serves to place him in the context of his profession: according to the prostitutes, now appropriately charac-

---

[3]See Joseph A. Fernández, 'Deformaciones populacheras en el diálogo galdosiano', *AG*, 13 (1978), 111-19, and Graciela Andrade Alfieri and J.J. Alfieri, 'El lenguaje familiar de Pérez Galdós y de sus contemporáneos', *Hispanófila*, no.22 (Sept. 1964), 17-73. Some of *Chanfaina's* phrases, whilst being enormously comic, show how Galdós, even at this level, could endow some of his words with relevance for the subsequent development of Nazarín's story. For example, she suggests that if he is mad, he should be sent to the 'manicómelo' to be fed. Scorning him as an 'alma de mieles' (I, ii; 17), she unconsciously suggests an association with her 'mieleros' clients. The 'tarascas' also exhibit a surprising linguistic talent, fashioning Latin phrases from the Mass into abusive epithets for Nazarín: '¡Vaya con el señor *Dominio vobisco*, asaltado por los ladrones!' (I, iii; 20). Galdós's use of popular speech was an important stylistic development in the nineteenth-century Spanish novel, although, in his prologue to the 1882 edition of *El sabor de la tierruca*, he duly acknowledged the pioneering achievements of his great friend, Pereda; see *Ensayos de crítica literaria*, ed. Laureano Bonet (Barcelona: Península, 1972), p.166. It is significant that Galdós blamed not only the purists of the Academy but also the Press for having prevented this development. At the end of his career, in 1915, he recalled in an essay, 'Guía espiritual de España' (*OC*, VI, 1507-08), the great difficulties he had in mastering the different categories of popular speech in Madrid.

terized as furious lionesses and panthers, Nazarín could enjoy a prosperous living if he said masses, funerals, baptisms (another verbal echo of the earlier 'fe de bautismo' y 'bautizaron' of the street name), like other clerics, who are also importantly viewed as tricksters: 'los curánganos, que no hacen más que engañar a la gente honrada con las mentiras que inventan' (I, iii; 19).

Perhaps influenced by these outbursts to qualify now his opinion of Nazarín's respectability as 'por lo menos aparente', the narrator watches his companion disperse the prostitutes before beginning the *interview* or 'interrogatorio'. The reporter had claimed that this journalistic technique would reveal Nazarín's history and character. Of the former, the reader is not much wiser after the narrator's elliptical reporting: 'supimos su edad, entre los treinta y los cuarenta, su origen, que era humilde, de familia de pastores, sus estudios, etc[...]' (I, iii; 22). As for his character, despite claims about the modernity of the technique (*6*, p.212), the format of the newspaper interview with its rapid, at times very brief, interchange of set questions and answers probes not so much Nazarín's character as his views on a host of contemporary issues. And as with the narrator, it is Nazarín's conviction about his views that strikes the reader: 'yo tengo mis ideas, las profeso con una convicción tan profunda como la fe en Cristo nuestro Padre' (I, iii; 21). His authority is his 'conciencia', yet Siona had been earlier described as the woman of 'más conciencia' in all Christendom. All of this stands in contradiction to an awareness that Nazarín shares with the narrator of the occasional deceit of language ('¡La propiedad! Para mí no es más que un nombre vano, inventado por el egoísmo', I, iii; 21) and of the need to adopt different perspectives on issues: 'si mira usted las cosas desde el punto de vista en que ahora estamos, claro que parece absurdo; pero hay que colocarse en las alturas, señor mío, para ver bien desde ellas' (I, iii; 21-22). As if to suggest doubt in the priest's own obedience to this injunction, *Chanfaina* now blocks the window with her voluminous body as she offers some eagerly received food.

The interviewers, relieved not to be facing the usual arrogance of interviewees, are sufficiently impressed by Nazarín's 'sencilla ingenuidad' to believe his declarations of orthodoxy, his conformity with his meagre existence, his social passiveness, forbearance and unashamed dependence on others for food, yet they fail to see how such a spiritual manifesto pales into insignificance beside the strident denunciation of all the works of the Printing Press, ironically delivered to two of its practitioners, who then reproduce it in print. By far the longest response from Nazarín, this self-consciously pedantic diatribe reaches its climax with the prediction that all printed works will eventually be recycled as manure for export to underdeveloped countries — ironically, that order will be given in a written legal decree. The reasons for Nazarín's aversion are worthy of note: true faith, and especially his own, does not need lessons from written memories of the past; divine revelation will show Humanity 'las verdades eternas' (an ironical counterpart to 'la eterna guasa de Madrid', perhaps). Moreover, books and newspapers, especially 'tanta novela mentirosa', tend to confuse and complicate issues: 'no hay que pedir a los libros ni mejor enseñanza ni nuevas ideas que confundan y enmarañen las que uno tiene ya' (I, iv; 25), for that would spoil the precision and order of Nazarín's most certain world picture. That he is appearing unrealistic and escapist in all this is evident from his rejection of the interviewers' offers to secure a post for him, and from his desire to dream of the ideal of poverty, which seems at odds with his subsequent assertion that modern scientific progress is regrettably producing more and more paupers. Only once is the authority of Christ cited — and then somewhat erroneously — when declaring that society's problems will be solved by the rebirth of the virtue of patience, the Lord's first and most beautiful commandment.

Ominously ironic comments and actions by the narrator bring this interview, now given a third designation, 'fisgoneo importuno', to a close: he is convinced that Nazarín is telling the truth, yet the negative formulation of that opinion and especially the use of the key word 'máscara' raises doubts: 'Lo dijo con tal candor y naturalidad, que no podríamos sospechar que le movieran a pensar y expresarse de tal manera ni el cinismo ni la afectación de humildad, máscara de un desmedido orgullo' (I, iv; 30). Furthermore, in words that recall the opening page of Part I, both narrator and reporter celebrate 'la feliz casualidad a que debíamos su conocimiento' (I, iv; 30). Chance, fortune and its sudden reversals are responsible not only for the meeting that gives rise to the novel but also for the formulation of opinions and phrases. Incredibly, after Nazarín's expressed wish to become even poorer, the two interviewers decide to leave him some money; but not only are they 'incapaces de calcular las necesidades de aquel ambicioso de la pobreza' (I, iv; 30), they do not look at the silver coins they surreptitiously leave behind. Yet the narrator declares unhesitatingly that it was a 'corta suma, que en total pasaría de dos duros sin llegar a tres' (I, iv; 30).

Given such unconscious obfuscation, how reliable and revealing are their subsequent verdicts on Nazarín? The reporter now breaks out of his former polite wonderment and in abusive tones reminiscent of *Chanfaina* and the 'tarascas' and with a similar final solution (confinement to an 'asilo'), he bitterly denounces Nazarín as a hypocrite and a social parasite who has made an art out of begging. And having confidently asserted before the interview that it would reveal Nazarín's character, he now — with equal conviction — believes that Nazarín has no character at all. But he almost totally destroys the credibility of these views with his climactic defense of the Printed Word, as absurdly comic as Nazarín's attack (I, v; 32).

Equally surprising is the narrator's sudden shift of opinion: eschewing conviction statements, he now wisely counsels moderation and patience in passing judgement on the priest: more time and observation are needed: 'No nos precipitemos, amigo mío, a formar juicios temerarios, que la realidad podría desmentir[...] Por mi parte, no me atrevo aún a opinar categóricamente sobre el sujeto que acabamos de ver' (I, v; 30). Putting words into practice, he now receives evidence from *Chanfaina* and the old gypsy in the patio: both confirm that the priest is a saint out of place in the modern world, where he should work for his living instead of allowing what little he possesses to be taken by those who seek his help. However, neither testimonial provides the narrator with the new evidence he wants, and both could be considered as self-serving, the speakers anticipating the interviewers' question before it is asked. In the case of the old gypsy his hyperbolic designation of 'don Najarillo' as 'el príncipe de los serafines coronados' (I, V; 34), is perhaps due to his intuition that the two visitors have given the priest some money which might end up in his hands. The narrator is then reminded by the 'máscaras' at the brandy stall that, even if his newly-found perspectivism and moderation are admirable, definitive judgements are not necessarily easy to reach. Soon, in fact, the narrator is reverting to his usual contradictoriness: returning to central Madrid and what he thinks is 'otro pueblo de mejor fuste' (I, v; 34), he still has to acknowledge that the importunate 'máscaras' are found everywhere. There can be no oasis of certainty and truth in the 'eterna guasa de Madrid'.

The two men spend the rest of the day talking about 'el singularísimo y aún no bien comprendido personaje' (I, v; 34), but they soon forget about him, although the narrator then adds disconcertingly that there were whole days when he thought only about Nazarín and engaged in a constant reappraisal, somewhat belittled by a toy comparison, that is the result not of new information, as he had earlier prescribed, but of his own limited experience. Despite his self-questioning, the narrator displays signs of his previous tendency to believe in absolute and definitive positions: has he created 'un Nazarín de nueva planta' (echoing perhaps the 'periodista[...] de nuevo cuño' at the novel's opening) or managed to 'posesionarme intelectualmente del verdadero real personaje' (I, v; 34-35)? His reply is exemplary: 'No puedo contestar de un modo categórico' (I, v; 35).

If the narrator had ended Part I at this point, he could then have convinced the readers of the underlying lesson about how to read the novel and illustrated his cautionary pictures with his own tentative readjustment. But to expect such a neat and definitive change of approach would belie the essential point of the text's message and the fitfulness of the narrator's mind. In another sudden lurch of direction the narrator raises questions and doubts about the rest of the text, which, if it is not a 'verídica historia', like Part I (I, i; 10), is an 'invención' (the reporter had referred to Nazarín's 'maravillas de inventiva' in refining the art of begging, I, v; 31). And such works present 'una ilusión de la realidad', perhaps another literary trick to be inserted in the 'eterna guasa de Madrid'. Paradoxically, this trick is termed a 'virtud', and it is a double virtue, for, in a surprisingly modern awareness (*29*, *32*, p.66), the narrator sees the novel as a joint product of the writer's 'arte expeditivo' and the reader's 'credulidad'. But having established that joint process, characteristically the narrator subverts it by wondering if there could be other writers of the novel beside himself. Again characteristically, this question is represented as the words of others, yet the oath '¿quién demonios?', recalling the same oath he had uttered on the opening page, suggests that it is the narrator's own self-questioning. He does not pause to consider the improbability of the other candidates (the reporter, *Chanfaina* or the old gypsy, *4*, p.121), nor the nonsensical meaning of his sentence, 'yo mismo me vería muy confuso si tratara de determinar quién ha escrito lo que escribo' (I, v; 35). But in this 'texte volontairement énigmatique' (*9*, p.455) even this one verb 'escribir' in its two conjugated forms may have two distinct meanings: invention/composition and transcription, respectively, that is to say, the narrator might mean that he is only transcribing something that somebody else has composed. But it is impossible to decide; we can only note the possibility of the ambiguity or the contradiction. Even in the final sentence of Part I the narrator still wilfully confuses the readers as he now authenticates the truth of the rest of the novel, if not its narration, but all without any evidence or justification (*1*, p.293; *4*, p.114). He fails to realize that the narrator of any novel cannot conceal himself: he is present, visible in every word of his text. Furthermore, if the narrator of Part I can vouch for 'la exactitud de los hechos' or the precision, clarity and sincerity of the rest of the novel, then that must mean that the rest of the work is a 'verídica historia'. But the narration is also 'nutrida de sentimiento de las cosas' (I, v; 35), which implies a poetical, subjective dimension. From the beginning to the very end of Part I, the narrator has succeeded in baffling us and preventing us from drawing any definitive conclusions about places, people's appearances or beliefs, but above all, about the words that he writes on the blank page and which constitute the text. The truth of the latter is simultaneously affirmed and questioned.

2 *Parts II-V: The History of Nazarín*

The concluding paragraph of Part I instantly disrupts the established reading sequence of the novel by posing two important questions: i) are the remaining parts a separate entity, detachable from the first? and ii) are they the work of a different narrator? In many ways Part I is a prologue, an 'advertencia al lector', and as such, eminently detachable. Yet, typographically, no separation is made: Parts II-V belong to the same whole as Part I, whatever their generic differences. Inevitably, then, an all-pervasive ambiguity surrounds the rest of the novel, the outer casing and its constituent elements, conditioning all evaluations of words, characters and events. On the one hand, there is absolutely no direct cross-reference to the important methodological lesson of Part I or even the narrator's sense of total bewilderment on his visit to Nazarín's dwelling. On the other hand, however, the plot of the novel will unfold as a direct result of those few incidents and events which occurred in Nazarín's room in Part I. Furthermore, the interview between the priest, the reporter and the narrator will be significantly paralleled by other equally important ideological interrogations of Nazarín in Parts III and IV. The narrator had also exhibited an intense interest in *Chanfaina*'s exceptional premises and its occupants, in addition to Nazarín, so that often the centre of his narrative attention seemed hard to fix. The 'historia verídica' of Nazarín will be no less diffuse in its focus, although Nazarín remains its titular centre.

a) Structure and Chronicler

Structure

Part II: Nazarín meets again one of the prostitutes seen in Part I, Andara, who takes refuge in his room one night after a bloody fight. When discovered by *Chanfaina*, she decides to set fire to the room, destroying all evidence of her stay. Nazarín accepts the hospitality first of a fellow priest and his mother, and then of some elderly friends who live close to the city limits.

Part III: Unable to gain work in the churches of Madrid because of his protection of Andara and some suspicion of involvement in the arson, the priest decides to go into the countryside begging and suffering hardship in imitation of Christ. He is soon joined by Andara and, after his seemingly miraculous cure of a dying child in Móstoles, by another female admirer, Beatriz. Nazarín's principal adventure in the novel is the long interview with the rural aristocrat, Belmonte, who believes that he is an Armenian bishop wandering Europe disguised.

Part IV: After more minor incidents testing their physical and spiritual stamina, the trio of itinerant beggars are taken prisoner by the Civil Guard on the orders of the Madrid judge. Beatriz's former lover, Pinto, unsuccessfully tries to prevent her march through her home town of Móstoles as a prisoner in the chain-gang of criminals. Nazarín is subjected by the arresting mayor to another lengthy interview on his actions and beliefs.

Part V: The chain gang continues its way to Madrid, with Nazarín the growing centre of conversation and the butt of ribald jokes and insults. Foregoing the chance either to escape or to retaliate, Nazarín contracts a fever and, as the party enters the streets of the capital, he believes Jesus speaks to him in a vision.

The arguable inclusion or exclusion of Part I from the structure of the novel as a whole gives rise to a number of varied patterns.

In terms of their varying length, the five parts form a symmetrical pattern. Part 3 is by far the most extensive, with 52 pages (9 chapters) of the Alianza text forming the centre of the novel, the Belmonte episode. Parts II and IV are the next longest, with roughly equal space, 33 pages (6 chapters) and 47 pages (8 chapters), respectively. The opening and closing parts are by far the shortest: 26 pages (5 chapters) and 29 pages (7 chapters), respectively. So there is a gradual extension of coverage per part reaching a maximum length in the middle number only to recede correspondingly at the end. On the other hand, if Part I is removed another arrangement develops: Parts II and V now become roughly equal in terms of pages (though not in number of chapters), whilst Parts III and IV have roughly equal prominence as the most extended sections.

If the novel is built upon the traditional literary theme of the opposition between the city and the countryside, between 'corte y campo', then Parts I and II, which take place in Madrid, contrast with Parts III-V, which occur in the countryside around the capital.

Another binary opposition — between activity and passivity — is proposed by Kronik (7, pp.84-85). Part I is an expository prologue, Part II constitutes a preparation for active movement; Part III and the first half of Part IV contain active movement while the second half of Part IV and Part V describe passive moment.

Ziolkowski (33, p.71) interprets Part I as a theoretical introduction to the character of Nazarín, his personality and his brand of Christianity, with Parts II and III consisting of picaresque adventures, and Parts IV and V relating the Passion of Nazarín.

If divisions are made according to novelistic sub-genres, then Parts I and II could be regarded as a contemporary naturalist novel with the emphasis on the detailed description of low-class locales, characters, and events, all connected in a network of relationships, and Parts III-V as the revival of the medieval chivalresque romance (through *Don Quixote*?), with a priest-hermit replacing the knight errant meeting all sorts of strange individuals (34, p.280). All of these structural divisions are valid in themselves and accord well with the multiple perspectivism encouraged by the methodological lesson of Part I.

Yet perhaps an even more complicated pattern can be superimposed on these divisions. Kronik (7, p.95) was right to note that '*Nazarín* en total es circular en la trayectoria de su acción': Nazarín is

gradually forced by the reality of events to leave the epicentre of his
room at *Chanfaina*'s boarding house and to move to the outskirts
before sallying forth into the countryside. After reaching his most
distant point at the castle of Méntrida/Aldea del Fresno, he is
returned, at a quicker pace, to the centre of Madrid and to another
establishment, a sanatorium. A further division could be made
between Part I and the others, if one considers the circular movement
of the narrator and the reporter in their gradual advance through
patio, kitchen, and corridor to Nazarín's room and their subsequent,
more rapid, return to their homes in central Madrid, as anticipating
the trajectory of the adventures in Parts II-V.[4]

The Chronicler

A multiplicity of narrators had been suggested for Part II-V, but in
reality there seems to be only one voice speaking in the rest of the
novel; there are no revealing words to indicate that *Chanfaina* or the
old gypsy are miraculously responsible for the remaining text. Nor
do any of the reporter's biting criticisms of Nazarín reappear to
suggest that he has written the chronicle. Having mischievously
played with the reader's expectations, Galdós seems to have returned
to the original narrator of Part I. Yet we can never be totally sure, for
the chronicler, as we shall call him, never refers back to his previous
experience or opinions of the priest. On the other hand, the chronicler feels no compulsion to explain his presentation of 'el buen
Nazarín' or 'mi hombre' (II, i; 39) at the beginning of Part II. Indeed,
the first words of the *History of Nazarín* have the same incomplete
precision of certain information given in Part I: 'Una noche del mes
de marzo' (II, i; 39). However, though he is not sure of the exact time

---

[4]The circularity of movement in the novel is underscored by the presence of
the *noria* in two locations: at the entrance to Móstoles and in one of
Belmonte's courtyards. Even in the countryside there are constant reminders
of the capital: not only are beggars making their way towards it, but others
like *Pinto* have to return with a herd of cattle. Belmonte's banquet table is
like those found in Madrid mansions. The services of Nazarín and his two
followers in the plague-ridden villages become superfluous with the arrival
help from the Government in Madrid.

Andara spends buying some matches, 'en poquísimo tiempo, que seguramente no pasaría de siete u ocho minutos' (II, iv; 58), he can be deadly accurate chronicling the various stages of the fire that she ignites: 'Al cuarto de hora de salir la diabólica mujer[...] A la media hora vieron que salían velloncitos de humo' (II, v; 60, 61). The chronicler is equally sure about the time Nazarín spends at the house of the 'cleriguito' (five days) and that of the old couple (three weeks).

Like the narrator of Part I, the chronicler displays an interest in onomastics: 'La tal Andara (a quien llamaban así por contracción de Ana de Ara)'; 'que Nazario (pues no siempre hemos de llamarle Nazarín, familiarmente)' (II, ii; 45). But there is no cross-reference to the discussion of names in Part I. The chronicler shows more concern with substitute designations for the priest, suitably varying a number of epithets according to the context; for example, when Nazarín escapes into the countryside he is called: 'el clérigo andante' (III, i; 79); 'el fugitivo' (III, ii; 81); 'el caminante' (III, i; 78). At the farm hut, he is referred to as 'el penitente' (III, ii; 84); 'el peregrino' (III, ii; 86); 'el asceta' (III, ii; 86). After his miraculous curing of the child at Móstoles, he is acclaimed by the other children in the village as 'el santo Nazarín' (III, v; 99). During his first instruction of Andara and Beatriz he is addressed by the chronicler as 'el buen maestro' (III, v; 101). During the encounter with Belmonte, the narrator's approval is even more evident: 'el gran Nazarín' (III, vii; 109); 'el buen peregrino' (III, vii; 111); 'el buen padrito' (III, vii; 112). For his unstinting service to Villamantilla he is called 'el heroico Nazarín' (IV, ii; 139). In Part V on his return to Madrid in the chain gang he is called 'el misterioso preso' and 'el desdichado sacerdote'.[5]

Although labelled a chronicle, Parts II-V contain a variety of literary styles. Part II opens with a lyrical description of a nocturnal

---

[5]Ujo will introduce a further contraction of Nazarín's name: 'tío Zarín' (IV, v; 157). Pinto is reported to call him 'un público moro' (IV, iv; 153) and 'el moro de los dátiles' (IV, iii; 144). The fat man in the arresting party addresses Nazarín as 'príncipe moro desterrado' (IV, vi; 165) whilst the mayor prefers the designation 'el moro Muza' (IV, vi; 164), a not inappropriate name, for it means a short cape worn by clerics or university graduates.

scene, more proper to the novel than the chronicle, and yet with
notes of obvious parody: 'Una noche del mes de marzo, serena y
fresquita, alumbrada por espléndida luna' Nazarín is gazing at 'el
cielo y la luna y las nubes blanquísimas, en cuyos vellones el astro
de la noche jugaba al escondite' (II, i; 39). At the same time the
description anticipates the far more serious game of hide-and-seek of
Andara. A similar parodic intent seems to lie behind the reporting of
the arson at *Chanfaina*'s, one of the staple items of the reporter's
columns, as outlined at the opening of Part I. There is a hybrid
mixture of confusing styles. The poetic phrases 'velloncitos de humo'
or 'la combustión era un júbilo del aire, que daba en obsequio de sí
mismo función de pirotecnia' clash with the frankly comical 'Apagar
tal infierno era imposible, ni aunque vomitaran agua sobre él todas
las mangas del orbe católico' (II, v; 61) or the familiar 'A última hora
trabajaron los bomberos para impedir que el incendio saltara a las
casas inmediatas, y, conseguido esto, aquí paz y después gloria' (II,
v; 62). Such hilariously minor details as the stealing of some animals
and the singing of the old gypsy's beard, and the repetition of the
rhetorical 'No hay para qué' to open two paragraphs, all serve to
confirm that the chronicler is quietly mocking the bombastic style of
contemporary journalism. Yet, at the same time, he is undermining
the authority of his own chronicle.

The chronicler's apparent omniscience is more energetically
conveyed than that of the narrator in Part I, if simply because he
does not immediately contradict himself. He creates momentary
suspense by witholding the identity of Ujo, for example (IV, iv;
152); he explains authoritatively why Nazarín should 'tutear' Beatriz
(III, v; 100); he also anticipates future events, indicating their
significance (IV, ii; 143). Like the narrator of Part I, the chronicler is
capable of employing currently fashionable anglicisms, as when he
terms the stoning of Nazarín's party by the children of Villamantilla
'este inocente *sport*, o *deporte*' (IV, ii; 140). His omniscience extends
even to the afterlife, when he confidently predicts that God will
forgive the trio the proud recounting of their heroism in Villamanta
'con mil y mil episodios patéticos que serían maravilla del mundo si
alguien los escribiera. Pero nadie los escribiría ciertamente, sólo en

los archivos del Cielo constaban aquellas memorables hazañas' (IV, ii; 141-42).

This last passage is important for a number of reasons. First, it is ironic that the chronicler, like the narrator of Part I, should fail to see that this account of the deeds at Villamanta has just been given, at least in part, by himself. The trio do have their 'historia': not just their oral report, but the chronicler's written version. Secondly, the assertion of a Heavenly archive with its chronicles of individuals' actions immediately adds a whole new dimension to the chronicler's *History of Nazarín* and the novel as a whole by postulating a higher, spiritual history, not written or printed with earthly materials, and which seemingly could cover the same life and events as the versions of the chronicler and the narrator. Furthermore, for the writing of that spiritual chronicle in Heaven, an earthly one, the Bible, is an acknowledged reference guide. Hence, Nazarín's chronicle, his 'historia verídica', can be related to other, more reliable and more accurate (for the Christian) texts.

As if to remind the readers, however, of the potential for mistake and confusion even in the most avowedly authoritative texts, the chronicler chooses this moment to refer for the first time to his documentary sources, not that these have been felt necessary, for the chronicler has written with uncontradicted authority to this point: 'Se encaminaron a un pueblo, que no sabemos si era Méntrida o Aldea del Fresno, pues las referencias *nazarinistas* son algo oscuras en la designación de esta localidad. Sólo consta que era lugar ameno y relativamente rico, rodeado de una fértil campiña' (IV, ii; 142) However, this first open reference to sources is disconcertingly imprecise: he calls them merely 'las referencias *nazarinistas*' (another neologism coined on the priest's name) without enlightening us as to the number of these sources, which thus form a hypothetical endless gallery of mirror texts within a text (chronicle) that is encased within a larger text (the novel *Nazarín*) and a possibly wider text (the Divine History of Nazarín). The citing of authority is not in order to resolve an ambiguity, but to confirm it as present in the books of authority themselves. The irony of this citation is that the confusion (not of name form as in chapter 1, Part I, of which we are reminded by the use of the word 'la designación') but of the identity of the village in question to which the trio has moved. The triviality of such documentary confusion adds an important corrective to the chronicler's reliability as the voice of total truth.[6]

This lesson is reinforced in Part V, towards the end of the chronicle and the novel, when the chronicler confesses difficulty in determining whether the prison at which the chain gang stayed was in Móstoles or not: 'Malísimo alojamiento tenían los infelices presos en Móstoles (o en dónde fuese, que también esta localidad no está bien determinada en las crónicas *nazaristas*' [yet another variant] (V, v; 201). But only two sentences previously the chronicler recorded their entry into the town. Typically, Galdós repeats his point with another example: the name of the prison is a misnomer 'pues la llamada cárcel no merecía tal nombre más que por el horror inherente a todo local dedicado al encierro de criminales' (V, v; 201). It is really a ramshackle structure in which the security òf the prisoners 'era un mito'. This is the expression of an 'exposición' (another written document) from a judicial body, 'la Junta penitenciaria', which is 'pidiendo al Gobierno fondos para construir cárcel de nueva planta' (V, v; 202).[7] The third and final example of linguistic confusion occurs when in the next breath the chronicler admits that he is not sure whether the prison in which Nazarín is housed still exists: 'La vieja, que no sabemos si existe aún' (V, v; 202). Placed in such close proximity to the talk about 'la nueva', the phrase deliberately sows confusion.

To these two important passages of source confusion can be added the chronicler's tour de force at the end of the narration when he reproduces directly the words of Jesus in Nazarín's vision. He

---

[6]His later declaration of a totally accurate transcription of the mayor's interview of Nazarín (el diálogo que a continuación puntualmente se transcribe', IV, vi; 166) is consequently suspicious.

[7]There are two other prisons mentioned in *Nazarín*: the one at Méntrida/Aldea del Fresno, according to the mayor, has bars which are the envy of those in Madrid. But it is really the prison at Navalcarnero that has excellent facilities, with separate areas for male and female prisoners. See *La Ilustración Ibérica* (27 April 1895) for contemporary Cortes debates on prison reform.

does this without a single word of explanation or qualification, as if
he were relating a normal occurrence. The chronicler, like the
narrator of Part I, thus ends his 'historia verídica' with an audacious,
seemingly unconscious, denial of the bases of his narration.
Throughout *Nazarín*, the certainty of the narrative voice is encased
within the uncertainty of the narrative technique: both the narrator of
Part I and the chronicler of Parts II-V do not fully realize the
implications of this opposition as they leave the readers to untangle
the web of truths, half-truths and untruths in what has been related.[8]

b. Nazarín's Historia verídica: *Words Versus Actions.*

Involvement with Andara and Beatriz

The opening description of *The History of Nazarín* continues the
picture of the priest presented in Part I: he is again seen as a somewhat sedentary, immobile person confined to his room in
Chanfaina's boarding house, except that now he appears more
meditative as he gazes at the moonlit sky. The note of parody in this
scene also extends to the figure of Nazarín, for the moongazing,
effected through misted window panes, and accompanied by an
indifference to the chimes of the neighbourhood clocks, is an escape
from reality and an excuse for daydreaming. But, as in Part I when
Chanfaina interrupted the exposition of his religious and philosophical ideals by appearing at his window with a plate of food, reality
once more intrudes when Andara interrupts his reverie by appearing
at the same window. The chronicler's familiar tones only add to this
deflation of the spiritual dreamer: 'Adiós claridad, adiós luna y adiós
meditación dulcísima del padre Nazarín' (II, i; 40). In the same way
that the narrator of Part I had difficulty initially in determining the

---

[8]After Nazarín's acerbic denunciation of printed works in Part I and his
suggestion that they be recycled as manure for export to underdeveloped
countries, there is irony in his wish now to end his days on a 'muladar'.See
Arthur Carl Holmberg, 'Louis Lambert and Maximiliano Rubín: The Inner
Vision and the Outer Man', *Hispanic Review*, 46 (1978), 119-36 (p.136), for
how this passage repeats some of Maxi's words as he enters the asylum of
Leganés at the end of *Fortunata y Jacinta*.

identity of Nazarín, so the latter now is not sure whether the shape at the window is a woman or not. The reader is once more reminded of all the lessons in Part I on the impossibility at times of correctly determining even observable physical reality, not to mention the far more difficult world of spiritual values. These echoes of Part I, unheralded by the chronicler, and amplified by Andara's reminding Nazarín of their previous encounter and by the comparison of her hushed voice to that of a 'máscara', disorient the readers somewhat, for having been led to expect perhaps a different type of Nazarín in this part of the text, they are forced to refer back to the images, words and actions of Nazarín already seen in Part I. Yet perspectives must change, for whatever reason, whether valid or not, as Andara now shows by acknowledging Nazarín as a saint 'porque es la realísima verdad' (II, i; 40) (although the next day when he is late in returning to the room, she experiences some doubt: '¡No sé, no sé..., porque unos le tienen por santo, y otros por un pillete muy largo, pero muy largo... No sabe una a qué carta quedarse', II, iii; 50). Andara's wounded condition forces the 'curita' to offer her 'la primera cura' (II, i; 42) and to stop his sermonizing on the need to repent. Nazarín is obliged by the reality of the moment to become a man of action as well as of words, with momentous consequences for the rest of the history and the novel (*12*, p.201), for the relationship between words and actions will to a large extent determine our assessment of the central character (*5*; *29*). This should not be seen as an opposition of terms, even at this initial point in the plot, for whilst Nazarín shows exemplary practical charity by tending her wounds and fetching her food the next day, he also offers wise spiritual advice about forgiving her assailant, La Tiñosa, as well as alerting Andara to the serious legal consequences of her fight.

Now acting the role of interrogator, the priest shows a natural desire to find out the truth of the matter: 'Cuéntame el caso liso y mondo[...] ¿Y cómo escapaste[...]? ¿Cómo conseguiste[...]? ¿Cómo pudiste[...] y por qué razón[...]?' (II, i; 43). Unfortunately, his subsequent decision to shelter her until the police arrive, if they do, is a compromise that is really an abdication of moral responsibility on his part, for on the one hand he is helping someone who needs his charity and, on the other, he will not hinder the course of justice. Because he is thinking only of his own moral self-satisfaction, he fails to realize that in legal terms he is an accessory after the fact and that his refusal to act properly will lead to greater complications. His irresponsibility becomes all the more evident when *Chanfaina*, uncovering Andara's hideout, warns him of the possible consequences of his choice of action. If before hearing her advice he had been only slightly anxious, he is now completely silent and quickly disappears for a convenient appointment with a colleague at the church of San Cayetano. By the time he returns, the house is ablaze but he shows no surprise or consternation: 'se le puso [a Chanfaina] delante el padre Nazarín, tan fresco, Señor, pero tan fresco, como si nada hubiera pasado, y con aspecto angelical le dijo: — ¿Conque es cierto que nos hemos quedado sin albergue, señora *Chanfa*?' (II, v; 62). The news of the loss of his own meagre possessions is greeted with a shrug of the shoulders and no sign of sadness. However, he does roll up his sleeves to generously help people move their belongings until late in the night. But once he is lodged at the house of his friend, the 'cleriguito', he forgets completely about Andara, the fire, and everything connected with the 'casa de huéspedes', as if these events were of no importance. Nazarín has lurched, suddenly and without warning, to the other extreme of self-interest. The fact is that in his friend's house he is well looked after and he can meditate to his heart's content.

Even when he is summoned by the magistrate to make a statement about Andara's case, Nazarín's principal concern is with his own image and with telling the truth only as it affects him. In Andara's plight he shows a faint-hearted, passing interest. His insistence on telling the whole truth (as he sees it) to the judge is prompted not only by his duty as a priest and by his conscience, but principally by an egotistical desire to please the legal powers and himself. His signature on the statement certifies his neat, clear-cut, but imperfect conception of the truth. In this self-satisfied escapism, which for Nazarín is following his conscience (26, p.94), he also fails to see the change of attitude on the part of the magistrate who, having initially treated him with the respect due to a priest, now watches him leave with a mixture of pity, scorn, and concern.

The contradictions in Nazarín's attitude and position are now the subject of local gossip and divided opinions, but Nazarín is impervious to this personal criticism, adhering to the doctrine (expounded in Part I) of accepting all insults and hardship with Christian forbearance. Only a trace of anger shows in his reference to the rumours as 'viles calumnias', and perhaps there is a little sarcasm when he refers to his friend's mother as 'la boñísima doña María de la Concordia' (II, vi; 66).

The conflicting actions and reactions of Nazarín continue during his subsequent stay with an old couple, the Peludos, in the Calle de Calatrava. On the one hand, he genuinely attempts — to no avail — to earn some money by saying masses at various churches in order to pay his lodging; on the other, he never asks his colleagues for an explanation of their hostility towards him nor does he follow the sound advice of an old cleric from the Vicar General's office that he explain the whole situation to his superiors frankly and openly. The news, however, that an official letter revoking his licence to preach and summoning him to the Bishop's office has been drawn up, is not conducive to any such rapprochement. Nazarín's response to the worsening situation is to avoid any contact that would involve a verbal examination, and to resort to one decisive act — physical escape into the countryside where he can realize his dream of living in poverty. But what his preliminary early-morning walks on the city outskirts show is that this decision is largely based on a sensory reaction to the beauty of Nature which is subsequently rationalized as a contempt for corrupt civilization. In reality he is escaping from the law and the Church, fulfilling a private wish to live alone: 'Se alejaba, se alejaba, buscando más campo, más horizonte, y echándose en brazos de la Naturaleza, desde cuyo regazo podía ver a Dios a sus anchas. ¡Cuán hermosa la Naturaleza, cuán fea la Humanidad!' (II, vi; 68)

The artificiality of this new existence is further confirmed by the removal of his clerical garb which 'le denunciarían por loco o malvado' (II, vi; 69), and by his rehearsal of walking barefoot in the mud of the patio when his sandals wear out (see *3* and *10* for different interpretations). In the circumstances, it is not surprising that the offer from Andara, through Paco Pardo who lives close by, of a clerical hat rescued from the garbage cans of a Madrid house, is met with an angry rejection by Nazarín; far more to his approval is the set of old clothes that his hosts now give him. He seems obsessed with appearing properly dressed for the part he is now going to play. The morning he abandons Madrid he firmly believes that he is escaping from a dark prison — ironically, his subsequent experience of real prisons in the countryside will lead to his greatest development as a person. But here, with his mind on God and looking at the sky, he believes he is entering a new land. This, however, is only the work of his excited imagination which 'centuplicaba los encantos de cielo y tierra, y en ellos veía, como en un espejo, la imagen de su dicha, por la libertad que al fin gozaba, sin más dueño que su Dios' (III, i; 75). Between the moongazing at the beginning of Part II and this skygazing at the beginning of Part III, Nazarín has not changed character very much: he is still a Romantic escapist who tries to ignore reality, and whose thoughts of God seem to take second place to his feelings of personal contentment. It is at this point that Nazarín finally confronts the implications of his action by arguing to himself that he is only following what the Voice of God ordered his conscience. At the root of his problem is his inability to accept that the word 'rebellion' ('tan feo nombre') can be applied to his case. He also seems to fear the words of censure ('la reprimenda') of his clerical superior and the 'dimes y diretes y vejámenes de una justicia que ni es justicia ni cosa que lo valga' (III, i; 75). His intoxication with this ideal ('embriagado, si así puede decirse, con la ilusión de la vida ascética y penitente', III, i; 76) prevents him from seeing that his claim of orthodoxy would have been more credible if he had stayed in Madrid to suffer the 'penalidades' he craves for, or to enter a house of lay members (tertiaries) of the Franciscan Order, as he now admits.[9] Nazarín shows commendable flexibility in viewing his

---

[9]The only other references to St Francis are to be found in Nazarín's talk to Andara and Beatriz about the saint (IV, ii; 141) and Belmonte's prediction that the new Messiah will be another St Francis (III, viii; 116).

actions from various perspectives, but he errs when he concludes, with what he thinks is 'la verdad bien depurada' (III, i; 76), that he is not guilty of insubordination to his ecclesiastical superiors. The clinching argument, of course, is that this new life has been ordained by the Voice of God in his conscience, but this is really a cover for his own wishes: 'escojo esta vida porque es la más propia para mí' (III, i; 77).

The voices of Paco Pardo and Andara, which temporarily delay him from performing 'el estreno de sus cristianas aventuras' (III, ii; 81) or 'su flamante oficio de pordiosero' (III, ii; 82), represent the jolt of reality intruding into the priest's fantasies. By calling her 'mala, corrompida', Nazarín hopes to stop Andara following him. When she does succeed in joining him (and, as later with Beatriz, Nazarín imposes as his condition obedience to his will and word), more harsh insults allied to rhetorical self-abasement greet her pleas that he cure the sick child of a friend who lives in Móstoles. When Nazarín agrees to visit the village, words of another kind — prayers to God — are now uttered by the priest to secure the child's recovery, yet the emphasis is on the suffering he hopes God will give him for this mercy: 'todo, todo sea para mí' (III, iii; 91). The female listeners, who have no means to know the real intent of his words, now believe totally in his power to work miracles because he says the prayers so convincingly (*14*, p.236). The use of an incendiary image suggests that the effects of Nazarín's words might have consequences as dangerous as those of Andara's act of arson.

If words that sound right have the desired effect, so do actions that appear to be authentic: when Nazarín puts his hand on the child's forehead for a while to feel her temperature, this is regarded as the crucial act of faith healing that for the child's mother confirms Nazarín's status as a second Christ. Indeed, the restoration of the child's health is miraculous, but Nazarín's responsibility for it is only apparent and coincidental. The women misread the meaning of his words and deeds. But does this misinterpretation really matter when the most pressing need — the recovery of the child — is achieved?

The same comment could be also applied to a consequence of this episode, Beatriz's joining the group. On the one hand, her previous association with Pinto and the probability of his pursuit of her, as well as her proneness to hysterical fits, suggest that her company will create problems that Nazarín should foresee. On the other hand, there can be no doubt that she is sufficiently attracted by Nazarín's Christian example and teaching to want to change her life and follow him. It is significant that when Nazarín teaches Christian doctrine to the two women, his language is free of rhetoric: he expresses ideas with enough clarity for the two women to understand and remember them. This is all admirable and positive, but Nazarín yearns for actions that will involve more hardship and suffering. A visit to Belmonte, who has a reputation as a local tyrant, will provide this experience. But contrary to what he expects and imagines at every minute of the visit, all Nazarín receives is a barrage of questions and statements to which he is obliged to give lengthy but fruitless rebuttals. Words once more take precedence over actions.

The Belmonte encounter

This episode, by far the longest and most important in the novel, forms the central panel of a triptych of interviews, all apparently designed to shed light on the enigmatic character and beliefs of Nazarín. Unobtrusive but detectable parallels of certain details with the first of those interviews are now traced by the chronicler. Nazarín's appearance, which to the first interviewers had seemed that of a 'moro manchego', is now totally Arabic, with his long black and white beard and tanned face. The designation of his former clerical garb, of which he is now free, as a 'máscara' reinforces the echo of the first interview. From a distance, the tower on Belmonte's estate (which dwarfs the neighbouring village of Sevilla la Nueva) stands out like a monastery's belfry. Could this, indeed, be the house of the Franciscans that Nazarín had promised to enter if he found one on his path? The religious appearance is not inappropriate in view of the subsequent interview between Belmonte and Nazarín, but its importance for our argument here is that the tower is not what it appears to be: it is in fact a dovecote, an appropriate structure for its owner, whose mind is later described by Nazarín as a birdcage. The tower could be equated with the street name of La calle de las Amazonas, as both initial indicators are misleading, though not totally so in retrospect. Just as the narrator and reporter had to traverse (and later re-cross) a series of spaces (patio, kitchen and corridor) to reach the epicentre of their attention, the dining-cum-living room of the priest, so now the latter is escorted forward (and later back) by Belmonte through two patios (one with sheep and cows, in contrast to the gypsies' asses of Part I) and finally towards his banquet room. Adjacent to this central space are a newspaper library (a counterpoint to Nazarín's meagre library of three books, reminding us also of his strictures against all forms of printed works) and a portrait gallery, which mirrors the few religious prints in Nazarín's bedroom. In his inability to comprehend the meaning of the portraits of Pope Pius IX and the saints, as well as scenes from the story of St John the Baptist's ordeal at Herod's court, Nazarín is experiencing the same bewilderment that the narrator of Part I experienced before the 'mil fantásticos dibujos' of *Chanfaina*'s portal or the 'irregularidad más que pintoresca, fantástica' of the patio's structures. Nazarín was in Part I the object of the verbal insults of the four 'tarascas'; now he is physically attacked by real wild animals, the guard-dogs. Furthermore, if a debatable crime (Siona's theft) initiates the interview in Part I, so in the second, Belmonte leads off with a question about another bizarre, though hypothetical, crime: 'Dime: si ahora te arrojara yo a ese pozo, ¿qué harías?' (III, vi; 108).

As the narrator of Part I had his curiosity aroused by preliminary information from the reporter, so now Beatriz's relation of conflicting opinions about the strange character of Belmonte spurs Nazarín forward. As the narrator and reporter returned to their central Madrid home to discuss the interview, so Nazarín later rejoins his female companions to report the details of his visit to the ogre of La Coreja. In both cases, the interviews are far from being illuminating about their subject. The narrator of Part I will need to gather more information from *Chanfaina* and the old gypsy. Nazarín, who had been told before his visit that Belmonte was an evil man, that he drank to forget his personal troubles, that he had killed his wife and been incarcerated on his estate by his relations, now hears additional variants from an old woman of the neighbourhood, la señá Polonia: that Belmonte, after much travelling in the Orient (Belmonte himself had earlier told Nazarín that he had been a consul in Beirut and Jerusalem), had returned home only to lose his sanity by an excessive study of religion; that he was a gourmand and a womaniser (also admitted previously to Nazarín), but that he has a good heart. The Belmonte interview, then, like the first one, for all the exchange of words, does not succeed in revealing the total truth about the participants: disorientation and perplexity are the common consequences.

These parallels are numerous and deliberate, even extending to such minor details as the comic interruption of Nazarín's pompous-sounding remarks on spiritual problems, in the first example by *Chanfaina*'s offer of food and in the second by Belmonte's devouring of his meal and raising his glass to Pope Leo XIII as Nazarín speaks. But the duplication of detail is not overtly rigid and exact. Indeed, there is one important difference between the two interviews: in the first, the visitors are the narrator and reporter, in the second, Nazarín, but the latter is still the subject of the interview, as Belmonte directs all his attention to the priest and Nazarín is forced on the defensive: he has to talk about himself rather than receive physical abuse from Belmonte. Nazarín and his beliefs are still the centre of the chronicler's focus, but it is his puzzled reaction to the bizarre character of Belmonte that catches our attention. In his inability to correctly appraise the country squire, Nazarín is only reflecting the response of those like the narrator, reporter, or the Madrid judge to his own enigmatic character. The irony is, of course, that Nazarín never perceives this parallel.

Belmonte, despite the portrait of his imperious appearance, reveals his personality through his voice, and as with Nazarín himself, it is the voice rather than the external appearance which makes the initial confirmation of personality for the visitor (narrator of Part I and Nazarín, respectively). The interesting titbits of rumour about Belmonte's background and character are not developed, as they would have detracted from his principal function of serving as a forceful sounding-board and prompter for Nazarín's statements on

socio-religious problems and the identity of the world leader who
will resolve them. The mutual staring at each other underlines their
basic similarity: a readiness to make judgements on the basis of
external appearance of people or the mere sound of their words
('conozco yo bien a mi gente[...] ¡Si tengo yo un ojo!' III, vi; 107),
the squire claims. Belmonte listens to Nazarín's sensible and
authoritative words not because he is interested in them *per se*, but
because he wants confirmation of the idea that has already formed in
his mind on seeing Nazarín — first sown by foreign newspaper
reports — that Nazarín is an Armenian bishop, Esrou-Esdras, who,
to fulfil a vow he made on the successful reintegration of his sect
within the Roman Catholic Church, is travelling incognito across
Europe and living humbly in the company of two noble ladies. The
newspapers are his indisputable source of authority: '¡Pero si tengo
aquí los periódicos que hablan del insigne patriarca y describen esa
fisonomía, ese traje, con pasmosa exactitud...!' (III, viii; 119).
Nazarín's strenuous denials of this identity are totally ineffectual:
Belmonte is obstinately certain of his judgement ('antes se dejara
desollar vivo que desdecirse de cosa por él sostenida y afirmada', III,
ix; 122), repeating his appeal to the authority of journalism. The
chronicler of Parts II-V thus continues the lessons assembled in Part
I: Belmonte's unshakable conviction about Nazarín's identity is as
patently absurd and faulty as is the insistence of those who label
Nazarín as a saint or madman. Human truth is always much more
complex and multi-dimensional than newspaper interviews suggest
(and Galdós is undoubtedly criticizing contemporary journalism for
its claim to objective truth). Nazarín's energetic denials, whilst
admirably free of rhetoric and made with total sincerity, fail to
convince, because Belmonte is not prepared to listen and revise his
neatly uncomplicated assumptions. But it has to be admitted at the
same time that Nazarín confuses his defence by agreeing that his
speech and learning do not correspond to his appearance and that he
has not asked his superior's permission to adopt this life of penitence
(III, ix; 121). When he protests, 'Yo no disimulo nada; soy tal como
usted me ve' (III, vii; 113), Nazarín forgets that indeed he has
adopted a disguise — that of the itinerant beggar. Belmonte's

accusation of 'ficciones', 'farsas', 'cristiano disfraz', 'el disimulo' (III, viii; 118), words that all echo the ambience of Nazarín's dwelling in Part I, are not without some truth. Given also his experience in the Middle East as a diplomat, in familiar contact with Semites of all the three major religions (Christian, Jewish, Muslim), and the uncanny coincidence of some details of the two stories, Belmonte's conclusion is not so incomprehensible or unreasonable as it may first appear.

Nor does the squire's wild conclusion invalidate the seriousness of the two men's earlier conversation and their concern for spiritual matters. Evaluation of the whole episode is necessarily more complicated and somewhat contradictory. If Nazarín strikes a ridiculous pose with his absurd anticipations of martyrdom at Belmonte's hands, he commands admiration for the courage with which he rebukes the squire's harsh treatment of his servants and his excessive pride. Yet at the same time our admiration is tempered by his pedantically rhetorical style of speech and his assurance that he is guiding Belmonte to the truth.

Some of his answers to Belmonte's questions, like those he gave in the first interview, are manifestly contradictory, to the reader, even if not to Nazarín himself. Belmonte's first general question on 'el estado actual de la conciencia humana' should have been an ideal opener, given Nazarín's constant references to 'conciencia' as his source of divine authority. His mumbled aside is a hilarious deflation of authority that puts his subsequent long-winded exposition into proper perspective: '¡Ahí es nada la preguntita! — dijo Nazarín para su sayo —. Tan compleja es la cuestión, que no sé por dónde tomarla' (III, viii; 114).

Nazarín repeats the main argument he had made in the first interview: Humanity is tired of Modern Science and is returning to an interest in spiritual matters. For all the so-called progress, Humanity is worse off than ever: there are more poor and hungry people than before the advent of industry. If that is so, then Nazarín should welcome more scientific progress, for his own oft-proclaimed ideal is poverty. Likewise, in his prediction of the eventual reunification of the Christian sects and denominations in the twentieth

century, due in no small part to the achievements of the current
Pope, Leo XIII, he fails to see how his own small independent band
of believers does not contribute to this general trend.[10] Having
announced, in cliché phrases, the coming realization of this goal,
Nazarín rejects the possibility of the new Moses coming from the
worlds of philosophy and politics precisely because of their empty
word-games or rhetoric. Yet his prediction that the new leader will
be a Pope, is a 'corazonada, una idea de filosofía de la historia' (III,
viii; 116). Nazarín does not realize how he immediately contradicts
himself. His emphasis on how 'los ciegos deben ser llevados de la
mano por los que tienen vista' (III, viii; 116) so soon after his own
physical eyesight has been singularly unhelpful in deciphering the
meaning of Belmonte's physical appearance, cautions the reader to
question the certainty of his assertion: Nazarín gets carried away by
his rhetoric, and Belmonte's enthusiastic approval, 'Verdad, verdad,
todo verdad... poseerla, ¡qué dicha!... Practicarla, ¡dicha mayor!' (III,
viii; 117), as he stirs himself from a postprandial drowse and drink,
casts some ironic doubt on Nazarín's exaggerated wish to see all
hatred, tyranny, hunger, and injustice disappear from the world. The
crowning absurdity is Nazarín's persistence in believing in these
ideals, even if they are all wrong (III, viii; 117).

Belmonte's words are also full of contradictions: he may be
keenly interested, like Nazarín, in ideas and spiritual matters, but he
will always indulge his tastes for good food and drink, if no longer
for philandering. These vices are the toys needed by old age, an
allusion that calls to mind the mental games of the narrator with
Nazarín's character (at the end of Part I), whilst his recognition of the
existence of such perfect people as Nazarín for those less perfect as
'una suerte' reminds the reader that the whole novel is the product of
an 'humorada': chance is indeed an important agent in the novel's
plot, although logic, reason and preconceived ideas are important

---

[10]According to León Lopeteguí, *El Concilio Vaticano Primero y la unión de
los orientales* (Berriz, Vizcaya: Ángeles de las Misiones, 1961), p.93, the
active part played by the dissident oriental sects in the First Vatican Council,
called by Pope Leo XIII in 1870 to discuss Church unity as well as the
question of Papal Infallibility, was important.

too, as Belmonte himself has admitted. These contradictions in his character contribute to the general pattern of confusion in the book and at the same time, if they trivialize his earlier seriousness, they do humanize him, although not to the extent of turning him into a bumbler (5, p.107).

Before Nazarín reaches the high point of his emotional as opposed to spiritual maturity, he will have to undergo a series of hardships and tribulations, in a reversal of the series of fortunate episodes he has experienced before and during the Belmonte encounter. His first trial, helping those that are sick or dying of smallpox in two villages of similar name — Villamantilla and Villamanta —, is welcomed with the usual rhetoric-filled exhortation to his two companions. But before the trio reaches the first village, the sound of an angelus ringing over a beautiful landscape at sunset confronts them with a problem of interpretation: 'Los humos, las esquilas, la amenidad del valle, las campanadas, la puesta del sol, todo era voces de un lenguaje misterioso que hablaba al alma sin que ésta pudiera saber fijamente lo que le decía' (IV, i; 132). The landscape picture repeats the lesson of the Belmonte episode and those of Part I, namely, that single views of things and people are defective: they have to be complemented by opposing perspectives. Opposites have to be reconciled and accepted because they can and do co-exist. In terms of the development of Nazarín, his sincere words and inaction can co-exist and complement each other; just as his empty rhetoric can be united with his positive action, as he will shortly demonstrate in the two villages. The irony of this *exemplum* is that it is Nazarín who provides the interpretation of synthesis without seeing its applicability to his own life or beliefs. At first, in fact, he stumbles into this interpretation. Only when he has recovered his dialectical aplomb does he extrapolate the opposite interpretations of Andara (happiness) and Beatriz (sadness) to the higher planes of the human soul and its transcendental destiny. Nazarín's divine reading of the Book of Nature does have positive effects on the two women: they are slowly rediscovering for themselves important Christian teaching on loving one's neighbour and looking forward to the life everlasting.

The practical help Nazarín and his two followers give to the sick and dying of Villamantilla appears truly heroic and noble, despite the chronicler's exalted use of military imagery. The village mayor marvels at 'tanta diligencia y religiosidad', whilst the village doctor pays tribute to the zeal of these 'ángeles bajados del Cielo' (IV, ii; 139). The only discordant note is the mischievous stoning of the trio by village children. Nazarín has indeed performed valuable practical service to the communities, a perfect response to the realities of the situation. Hence, it is all the more regrettable that subsequently he reverts to his more usual dreaming of hardships (aptly conveyed in his moongazing atop the battlements of the old castle at Méntrida/Aldea del Fresno), ignoring the sensible advice of the women to escape before Pinto captures them. Yet despite all the religious rhetoric of these moments of dreaming, Nazarín's words to Andara and Beatriz at points of genuine crisis, as when they are harshly dismissed by the leader of the vineyard workers or attacked and robbed by two criminals disguised as Civil Guards, offer effective consolation and encouragement to bear the tribulations. Nazarín's words and actions are a strange mixture of effective practicality and well-meaning but empty rhetoric, for others, including the readers, if not for himself. When he repeats 'vuestro deber es la obediencia, el respeto a todo el mundo y la conformidad con los designios de Dios' (IV, vi; 162), he fully means it; his submission to arrest by the mayor of Méntrida/Aldea del Fresno now attests to the practice of what he preaches.

The Interview with the Mayor of Méntrida/Aldea del Fresno

The final part of Nazarín's journey is prefaced by the third panel of the triptych of interviews upon which the structure of the novel is built, according to one viewpoint. As with the preceding two, the main point of this final interview seems to be to give Nazarín an opportunity to expound his beliefs and the reader to judge them, or at least some of them, according to prior or subsequent action.

Now labelled as a 'diálogo' (IV, vi; 166), this interrogation is linked to its predecessors by a number of details. First, a journey is undertaken by the interviewee to the interviewing room, but, in contrast to what happens in the Belmonte episode, Nazarín is now forced to make that journey, which combines to a certain extent both the festiveness of the first made by the narrator of Part I and the apprehensiveness of Nazarín's visit to Belmonte when attacked by the dogs. The night party that accompanies the mayor is composed of men, women, and children, the last carrying blazing torches, and the noise they make is a mixture of laughter and jokes, as if it were an 'algazara de noche de San Juan' (IV, vi; 164). Both the mayor and the fat man in the party banter with Nazarín and the women, calling them names 'como si la libertad o prisión de gente tan humilde fuera cosa de broma' (IV, vi; 164). The chronicler becomes more explicit as the party returns to town: 'Por la cuesta abajo siguió la chacota y el escándalo. Más parecía aquello bullanga de Carnaval que prendimiento de malhechores' (IV, vi; 166). Yet the arrest is not without its serious moment of physical danger: like Belmonte's guard dogs, Andara now springs like a tiger with a knife on one of the bystanders. Despite his 'desmedida importuna afición a las bromas' (IV, vi; 166), the mayor and later some townsfolk (like Belmonte and *Chanfaina*), take pity on the party and provide them with food during the prison stay and for their march the next day. As with *Chanfaina*'s 'casa de huéspedes' and Belmonte's mansion, the nomenclature of a prison seems an error for it is only a stable with a grille, located in the lower half of the town hall, access to which is through a patio, with the interview taking place in an inner room beyond the room where the prisoners will be lodged for the night.

As with the two previous interviews, short question and long answer succeed each other in uninterrupted fashion, without comments by the chronicler, as if it were the text of a newspaper interview. Yet, contrary to what happened in the other interviews, it is not Nazarín but, increasingly, the mayor who makes the longest statements, revealing his distinctive character — unaccompanied by a physical portrait from the chronicler — in the process. There are good reasons for this shift from interviewee to interviewer: Nazarín has been arrested and is being interrogated by an official who could use the priest's words as evidence against him, although this

possibility would hardly trouble Nazarín. Secondly, as the mayor has
to review the charges against Nazarín, he has to speak at some
length, and again we are given Nazarín's full names, his status as a
priest (only believed because the warrant says so) and his appearance
as a Moor. However, the fundamental problem is that Nazarín does
not want to bother himself with the precise reality of the charges
against him: forever the escapist, he cannot confront reality honestly.
The charges, which constitute a sort of summary of the novel prior to
its dénouement, are serious (but, according to the mayor, a good
Madrid lawyer could obtain his release by arguing for insanity):

 a) that he gave sanctuary to a criminal, Andara;
 b) that they both set light to private property;
 c) that they both wander the countryside deceiving
 people with miraculous cures and preaching against the
 principle of private property.

Nazarín does not address himself to these specific charges, but is
merely content to pronounce a general refutation that is no more than
a repetition of some of the principles contained in the other
interviews. Thereafter, he replies only with short phrases, leaving all
the talking to the mayor, who is so nonplussed by the priest's persistent reticence that, in order to elicit information about his adventures
and miracles, he is compelled to try, with ever-increasing futility, all
sorts of ploys: bonhomie, hospitality, frankness, false modesty,
erudition, sarcasm ('la broma insolente, la befa y el escarnio', IV, vii;
171), all of which is appropriate given his character and the
importance of 'bromas' in the novel.

 Nazarín's silence forces the mayor to outline his own system of
materialistic values, which inevitably clash with those of Nazarín.
The latter is only half correct when he tersely indicates to the mayor:
'Señor mío, usted habla un lenguaje que no entiendo. El que hablo
yo, tampoco es para usted comprensible, al menos ahora.
Callémonos' (IV, vii; 171). Nazarín understands perfectly well what
the mayor is saying; it is the substance of his remarks, the ideas and
values themselves, which Nazarín cannot accept, for they are

anathema to him; but rather than tell the mayor so, he camouflages his antipathy, and the generic tag for language is used as the word of deceit.

The mayor extols the virtues of nineteenth-century progress: scientific inventions (the steam engine, the telephone and the printing press — by which he must surely mean mass book-printing) and the work ethic. The only difficulty in accepting the mayor's *apologia* for improving the material well-being of contemporary society (and he may well be right that Jesus would bless such advances, if He returned to Earth) and spurning the ascetic religious practices of the past is that his catalogue of practical social reform: degenerates into an absurd flight of fancy:

> He aquí el problema. Dar salida a nuestros caldos, nivelar los presupuestos públicos y particulares..., que haya la mar de fábricas..., vías de comunicación..., casinos para obreros..., barrios obreros..., ilustración, escuelas, beneficencia pública y particular... ¿Y dónde me deja usted la higiene, la urbanización y otras grandes conquistas? Pues nada de eso tendrá usted con el misticismo, que es lo que usted practica; no tendrá más que hambre, miseria pública y particular[...] El siglo XIX ha dicho: 'No quiero conventos ni seminarios, sino tratados de comercio. No quiero ermitaños, sino grandes economistas. No quiero sermones, sino ferrocarriles de vía estrecha. No quiero santos padres, sino abonos químicos.' ¡Ah, señor mío, el día que tengamos una Universidad en cada población ilustrada, un Banco agrícol? en cada calle y una máquina eléctrica para hacer de comer en la cocina de cada casa, ¡ah!, ese día no podrá existir el misticismo! (IV, vii; 170-71)[11]

---

[11]This sounds very much like a Socialist Party manifesto, but Galdós has carefully not included the three major tenets of the first manifesto of 1879 of the Spanish Socialist Party: abolition of classes; nationalization of private property; political power to be given to the working class — see Miguel

The chronicler's jesting comment on the sweat and 'dolores
partúricos' of this 'larga y erudita oración' (IV, vii; 171) as well as
the mayor's earlier tongue-tiedness on completing an idea reinforce
the comic shallowness of the mayor's readings as an erstwhile
seminary student. His half-remembered clichés of progressive
propaganda are a fitting match to Nazarín's spiritual rhetoric, each
apologist intolerant of the other's viewpoint, when there is some
right and some truth at the bottom of what each preaches. On the
other hand there is much to laugh at. The mayor is right — in part —
to ask Nazarín to dismiss his words as a 'broma, que a mí me gusta
darlas' (IV, vii; 172). Indeed, it is not the usual interrogation of a
prisoner by the authorities, but the conversation of 'dos amigos muy
guasones, un par de peines de muchas púas' (IV, vii; 173). Has the
interview served any purpose, then? Has it been any more than a
sterile exchange of empty rhetoric? As far as Nazarín's creed is
concerned, nothing new is gleaned; what the interview does reveal,
though, is the equally vacuous, though well-meaning, exposition of
ideals by an official representative of the society that Nazarín has

Artola, *Partidos y programas políticos, 1808-1936*, I (Madrid: Aguilar,
1974), p.504. It is also ironic that Nazarín should have praised Pope Leo so
highly in the Belmonte interview, for he seems to be ignorant of Leo's
efforts to improve working people's living conditions. In his most famous
encyclical, *Rerum Novarum* (1891), the Pope had clearly stated the Church's
duty to consider the material needs of Humanity (a view not shared by
Nazarín): 'Neither must it be supposed that the solicitude of the Church is so
preoccupied with the spiritual concerns of her children as to neglect their
temporal and earthly interests. Her desire is that the poor, for example,
should rise above poverty and wretchedness, and better their condition in
life: and for this she makes a strong endeavor.' Reproduced in Anne
Fremantle, *The Papal Encyclicals in their Historic Context* (New York: The
New American Library, 1956), p.179. The means to achieve these improve-
ments will be the practice of true Pauline charity (p.195), a word that is
never on the lips of Nazarín. In 1894, there had been a large pilgrimage of
Spanish workers to Rome and Pope Leo had exhorted the Spanish bishops to
establish Catholic working men's assocations to counteract the rise of
socialism; see James McCaffrey, *History of the Catholic Church in the
Nineteenth Century (1789-1908)* (Dublin: M. H. Gill, 1910)), II, pp.386-88,
and Ferdinand Brunetière, 'Après une visite au Vatican', *Revue des Deux
Mondes*, 127 (1985), 97-118.

spurned and which is now going to judge him. Given the values of contemporary society, as expressed by the mayor, how wrong — or right — is Nazarín to have said and done what he has? The point surely is that the spoken or written word, when not accompanied by corresponding action, lacks conviction, or as Galdós would say in a later novel, *El caballero encantado*, 'cuando la palabra no tiene dentro la obra del varón, es hembra desdichada, horra y sin fruto' (*OC*, VI, 256).

In the final stage of Nazarín's journey in the countryside, words and action will be fused harmoniously — but only for a short while. The practical example to accompany the foregoing theory of the interview is seen in the tribulations Nazarín has to endure from his fellow prisoners of the chain gang on the road to Madrid or in the prisons of Navalcarnero and Móstoles. Like Belmonte and the vineyard workers, the prisoners invent all sorts of stories about the background of Nazarín and the two women. The climax of this 'estúpida y repugnante bufonada' played out in Navalcarnero jail is the order that Nazarín should celebrate a Black Mass. At this point, Nazarín's anger is aroused and he refuses to follow the order, an action which is accompanied by a summons to the criminals to repent and love their neighbours. The style of his speech is still heavily rhetorical but it no longer completely cloys or bores. The words have some real meaning in this context because they correspond to Nazarín's genuine concern for the sinful men. However, when he identifies them with the persecutors of Christ, his words start to lose conviction. It is perhaps not without significance that this speech is framed against a moonlit window: in similar scenes earlier in Parts II and III, Nazarín had always been portrayed as the engrossed, silent meditator. Now his meditations are voiced and directed towards an audience of sinners, and if their expression is still stilted, they will have a magnetic effect on one of the listeners, *El Sacrílego*, who will be converted by these words and join Nazarín's band. The lunar halo would seem now to be justified.

The reaction of another criminal, *El Parricida*, to this speech is to brutally assault Nazarín. This is the apparent turning-point in the novel, when Nazarín the idealist reveals himself to be also a man of

flesh and blood: 'Era hombre, y el hombre, en alguna ocasión, había
de resurgir en su ser, pues la caridad y la paciencia, profundamente
arraigadas en él, no habían absorbido todo el jugo vital de la pasión
humana' (V, i; 186). The man of passion forgets his ideals and their
rhetoric; words now give way to sighs and groans and he arches like
a cat as he rises. However, he slowly overcomes the natural desire
for revenge by reasserting the supremacy of Christian forgiveness.
His speech is now shorn of the stylized phrases of the first oration
and meets with the chronicler's approval: words are now matched by
action, which, paradoxically, is a deliberate rejection of other action:

> La respuesta al ultraje fue, y no podía menos de serlo,
> entre divina y humana.
> — Brutos, al oírme decir que os perdono me tendréis por
> tan cobarde como vosotros..., ¡y tengo que decíroslo!,
> ¡amargo cáliz que debo apurar! Por primera vez en mi
> vida me cuesta trabajo decir a mis enemigos que les
> perdono; pero os lo digo, os lo digo sin efusión del alma,
> porque es mi deber de cristiano decíroslo... Sabed que os
> perdono, menguados; sabed también que os desprecio, y
> me creo culpable por no saber separar en mi alma el
> desprecio del perdón. (V, i; 187)

But then there is a sudden change of narrative tone: all the other
criminals, except *el Sacrílego*, fall on Nazarín, but it is not a serious
attack at all, more of a joke, 'una burla pesada y brutal', 'las bárbaras
y descomedidas burlas', 'las chanzas brutales', 'infame juego', with
'risas burlescas' (V, ii; 187-88). The real gravity of *El Parricida*'s
attack and the nobility of Nazarín's response give way at first to a
more confused mixture of aggression and farce, and finally end on a
completely comic note when the chronicler reports the loud snores of
the old beggar, perhaps dreaming of his large inheritance from a
brother in South America. In the constant shifting of narrative moods
and tones, it is not surprising that in the next paragraph Nazarín
restores the note of seriousness by once more urging the criminals to
repent and by offering his life to achieve this act of contrition.

Indeed, he begins to have some effect on his audience — as a new silence descends on the cell, consciences are slowly stirring and *El Sacrílego* now publicly declares the goodness of Nazarín, standing ready to defend him against all attackers.

As the *History of Nazarín* and the novel as a whole draw to an end, the priest is conveniently stricken with a fever, which considerably distorts his normal appreciation of physical space, time, and speech. He first experiences this sensation in the prison at Móstoles when he sees Andara in his cell and hears her talking to him, but the images, visual and oral, are blurred. In this abnormal state words no longer have reliable meanings for Nazarín, as he prefers to trust his other physical sense of sight (the verbal form 'vio' is repeated three times in one paragraph, V, v; 204) and touch. Yet the words of Andara and *El Sacrílego* urging him to escape with them through a hole in the roof of the prison are clearly intelligible; but because the suggestion goes against his principle of resignation, he cannot believe what he is hearing. Typically, though, he has no doubt whatsoever that he told them he was not going to escape. The typhoid attack only puts into relief the character of Nazarín as seen in the rest of the novel: he is a man who cannot see his own contradictions.

The fever causes a total distortion of phenomenal reality the following day when Nazarín sees Beatriz, Andara and *El Sacrílego* as transfigured actors in a medieval allegorical battle against an enemy host. (Ironically, Nazarín had earlier ridiculed Beatriz's visions as products of sick people's nervous imagination.) The vision clearly shows Nazarín's attraction to and interest in the bodies of the two women (with very little appreciation of their spiritual values): Beatriz is a celestial beauty, Andara, an Amazon warrior of dynamic energy, the Church contemplative and the Church militant respectively, perhaps. Yet the narrative style employed by the chronicler is so exaggeratedly literary that in the description of Andara, for example, it almost turns the vision into pure comedy: ' Vestida de armadura resplandeciente, en la cabeza un casco como el de San Miguel, ornado de rayos de sol por plumas, caballera en un corcel blanco, cuyas patadas sonaban como el trueno, cuyas crines al viento parecían un chubasco asolador, y que en su carrera se llevaba medio mundo por delante como huracán desatado' (V, vi; 207). The chronicler also mimics the tripartite sentence structure so favoured by Nazarín in his perorations, but now in referring to Nazarín himself: 'venía contra él, contra el santo, contra el penitente, contra el oscuro mendigo[...] ¿Podría ésta al fin destruir al santo, al humilde, al inocente?, (V, vi; 207). Before Andara slaughters the *antinazarista* host - counterpoint to the equally nebulous account, given at the beginning of the novel, of sixteenth-century Amazon prostitutes welcoming Isabel de Valois to Madrid — she harangues the enemy: 'Atrás, muchedumbre vil, ejército del mal, de la envidia y del egoísmo. Seréis deshechos y aniquilados si en mi señor no reconocéis el santo, la única vía, la única verdad, la única vida. Atrás, digo, que yo puedo más y os convierto en polvo y sangre cenagosa y en despojos que servirán para fecundar las nuevas tierras' (V, vi; 208). In a novel that has consistently stressed the need to avoid single perspectives on any matter, Andara's hailing of her master as the only way, the only truth, the only life — an adaptation of Jesus' words in St John's gospel, 14:6 — is misguided and exaggerated, and somewhat mocked by her threats to turn the enemy to blood and dust that will fertilize 'las nuevas tierras' — possibly an ironic echo of Nazarín's prediction in Part I that in the future all printed works will be converted into fertilizer for export to under-developed countries. After the slaughter the chronicler appends a further comic note when describing the battlefield as covered with 'charcos de sangre y picadillo de carne y huesos' (V, vi; 208).

By the time Nazarín enters Madrid he has recovered from this fantastic vision, but his fever still prevents a totally clear appreciation of the surrounding physical and temporal reality: 'Dudaba entonces, como antes, si eran realidad o ficción de su desquiciada mente las cosas y personas que en el doloroso trayecto veía' (V, vii; 209). However, the monologue in which Nazarín, at the sight of a street cross, declines to imitate his Lord and yearns for a humble, totally obscure death, displays his customary stilted style, with its underlying false modesty: 'Soy el último de los siervos de Dios, y quiero morir olvidado y oscuro, sin que me rodeen las muchedumbres ni la fama corone mi martirio. Quiero que nadie me vea perecer, que no se hable de mí, ni me miren, ni me compadezcan. Fuera de mí toda vanidad. Fuera de mí la vanagloria del mártir' (V, vii; 209).Appropriately Nazarín's final physical sensations are of complete disorientation, unable to decide whether he is in the land of the living or of the dead. Nevertheless, a desire to communicate with God — here appropriately called 'la Suprema Verdad' — is immediately realized, or so it seems. However, it is the final irony of the novel that even this act, the elevation of the Host in the Mass, which the chronicler reports Nazarín as celebrating, is an illusion: the voice of Jesus, after telling Nazarín that he has been hospitalized and that his two followers are imprisoned, indicates: 'No puedes celebrar, no puedo estar contigo en cuerpo y sangre, y esta misa es figuración insana de tu mente' (V, vii; 210). To accept these words at their face value would be contrary to the reading methodology suggested for the whole work: the chronicler chooses to make no disclosure about how he is sure of this reproduction of divine words. Nevertheless, they contain their own contradiction: the voice of Jesus informs Nazarín and the reader that the former is not saying Mass (were those he was reported to have infrequently said in Madrid churches in Parts I and II any more real or true?), but the fact remains that, according to the words of the text of the chronicle/novel, Jesus does speak directly to Nazarín - if not in the Mass, in some form of divine communication. But then, would Jesus have called Andara and Beatriz 'las dos perdidas'? In addition, Jesus's purported last words do provide a most appropriate conclusion to this novel of total ambiguity: 'Algo has hecho por mí. No estés descontento. Yo sé que has de hacer mucho más' (V, vii; 210). Within their outer casing of uncertainty (made up of the questionable filters of the supernatural speech, Nazarín's feverish state and the chronicler's omniscient narration) these words, paradoxically, exude a certainty about the past ('Algo has hecho por mí') and the future ('has de hacer mucho más') and there is no doubt about the latter ('Yo sé'). Yet it must be noted that the Voice does not define what it means by 'algo' or 'mucho más'. Moreover, is the verb 'hacer' a totally correct choice to sum up Nazarín's achievements? What does it refer to? Surely, Nazarín has also said a lot and will say more for Jesus. Or does the verb 'hacer' include this meaning?

In its contradictions and imprecisions, this final phrase sums up the lessons of both Part I and Parts II-V, of prologue and history/novel: definitive conclusions about the accomplishments of Nazarín (or lack of them) are to be avoided. Contradictions and ambiguities have to be recognized and accepted as such. Nazarín's words and deeds achieve varying results: ideas may be expressed clearly (to Andara and Beatriz) or turgidly (to *El Sacrílego* and the other criminals), with equally or partially positive results. On the other hand, telling the honest truth (to Belmonte and the investigating magistrate) is totally unproductive in the first case, or counterproductive in the second. Likewise, some of his actions (helping the afflicted of Villamantilla) can achieve noble results, although for the wrong reason of self-suffering. At other times, the right actions, like giving food to fellow beggars (see Chapter 2d) produce negative results. Just as Nazarín expected, when he set off into the countryside, to live a life according to a preconceived plan, so the readers expected, on opening the novel, to read an uncomplicated story about a character called Nazarín. In both cases, the reality of the adventures is much more complicated, forcing both Nazarín and the readers to revise previous expectations. One of those revisions concerns the centre of attention in the novel: certainly Nazarín seems to be the protagonist, yet, because of his involvement with other characters and his effects on them, these characters — e.g. Belmonte and the Mayor — can take on unusual prominence and capture the reader's attention by the sheer force of their personality as expressed through their distinctive language. The same could be said with greater justification of Nazarín's two female followers.

c) *The Secondary Characters: Beatriz and Andara; Pinto and Ujo*

The one notable change in Nazarín's character is the affection he comes to feel for Beatriz and Andara as human beings. Having tried first to dissuade them, he allows them to accompany him: they do indeed force him out of the narrow egotistical confines of his religious mission (*13*, p.192). If to Belmonte he angrily denies their spiritual status ('Esas mujeres no son santas, sino todo lo contrario', III, ix; 124), he recognizes his feelings for both of them as they sit by the roadside before they are arrested: '¡Querer yo a la una más que a la otra! Si hay diferencia en el modo de tratarlas, diferencia fundada en el natural de cada una, no la hay en el cariño que les tengo' (IV, vi; 163). Living and travelling together, the three come to form a happy family group, arguing good-humouredly over, for example, who is to eat the egg Ujo had given Andara (IV, iv; 154), or sharing their fears (Beatriz's of Pinto, Andara's of Nazarín's preference for Beatriz). The result is that when in the prison of Navalcarnero Nazarín is separated from 'las nazarinas', as they are called by the other prisoners (V, i; 184) — another neologism built on the priest's name —, he feels as disconsolate as they do at prayer-time. Yet Nazarín is wrong to underestimate the effects of his teachings on the two women: they are influenced to a surprising extent by his words as well as by his personality. The result is that Beatriz and Andara become complex, enigmatic characters like Nazarín, in keeping with the essential texture of the book.

Beatriz

Andara brings Beatriz into the text when she energetically tries to persuade Nazarín to enter Móstoles to cure the sick daughter of Beatriz's sister, Fabiana. Beatriz is young and pretty enough to earn a living in Madrid, presumably as a city prostitute. Although she comes from the country, she has features (well-kept hands and earrings) that liken her to a city woman. These details justify Pinto's persistent attention and explain perhaps the rumours of sexual scandal about her association with Nazarín, as well as mirroring more important inner contrasts. Indeed Nazarín cannot believe that she is ill from merely looking at her; paradoxically, as Andara points out, she has looked prettier each day since her return from Madrid. In reality, Beatriz suffers the mental disorder of hysteria, an appropriate illness for this novel in that it is not constant but periodic and unpredictable. Furthermore, there are various symptoms: loss of sleep and appetite, epileptic fits, desires to kill her mother or devour a child, subsequent remorse, suicidal tendencies and an aversion from priests. There are conflicting opinions about its causes and cures: Fabiana believes that the illness is the result of evil spells cast by envious villagers, while for Andara, Pinto has given her a nervous breakdown. Only later does Andara reveal that Beatriz has had two miscarriages. Medication, varied and unsuccessful, has been generally of a rustic nature: herbs, insects and talismans. Nazarín's suggested cure is of a vastly different nature, which, if rather optimistic, is strikingly modern: Beatriz should convince herself that her illness is merely the result of her imagination and not of any organ damage; praying to God, eating and exercising will complete the cure.[12]

Nazarín's diagnosis of 'esas extrañas aberraciones de la sensibilidad que produce nuestro sistema nervioso' (III, iv; 94) — surprisingly modern in a person who elsewhere rejects the advances of science — is undercut by a number of comic notes: Andara had experienced something similar in puberty: her medication had been bromide, 'bromura' which she mispronounces as '*broma dura*', a verbal joke to add to the other examples of 'bromas' in the text. Beatriz also mispronounces the illness as 'esterismo', and finally there is some irony in Nazarín's diagnosis of an imaginary illness, when his principal weakness is imagining future torments and sufferings. Nevertheless there can be no doubt that Beatriz is soothed by his words, which also serve to control her next hysterical attack just before they arrive at Villamantilla: for the first time she

---

[12]The diagnosis of hysteria offered the same year by the psychiatrist, José María Escuder, *Locos y anómalos* (Madrid: Sucesores de Rivadeneyra, 1895), p.249, is remarkably similar: 'La histérica necesita algo extraño que hiera su imaginación, que sacuda y desaloje la idea paralítica.' Escuder was a colleague of Galdós's close friend, Manuel Tolosa Latour; see Joan Connelly Ullman and George H. Allison, 'Galdós as Psychiatrist in *Fortunata y Jacinta*', *AG*, 9 (1974), 7-36 (p.23). Zeda's review for *El Imparcial* (10 April 1895), of *Jesús de Nazareth*, a tragedy in five acts by the Catalan playwright, Angel Guimerá, describes the Mary Magdalene of the play as an 'endemoniada, una histérica, que más parece sujeta a la influencia de la sugestión hipnótica que a la tiranía de la pasión amorosa' (p.2).

experiences pleasant mental images after vibrations have rippled through her body. She is unable to explain or be sure of what she sees, but whether it is God, angels or 'un purísimo espíritu que quería tomar forma sin poder conseguirlo' (III, i; 135), the vision anticipates Nazarín's final vision and is likewise suitably reported in free indirect style.

The Villamantilla and Villamanta campaigns show 'la de Móstoles' (III, v; 100) to be practical as well as hypersensitive;[13] but her provident side had already been noted earlier when she had presented herself ready for a journey with the appropriate clothes and accoutrements (for example, matches). She will later show justifiable prudence in counselling Nazarín to avoid Belmonte's estate. Nevertheless, she has to overcome an understandable aversion from the misery of the infected villages and she does this by recalling words and ideas of her master. The employment of the metaphor of fire for her spiritual courage (IV, i, 134) inevitably recalls the real fire Andara had been inspired by Nazarín to start at *Chanfaina*'s 'casa de huéspedes'. And as Andara rejoiced watching the flames leap out of the building, so Beatriz draws some self-satisfaction and pleasure at her performance: 'en sí misma, en su aprobación interior y en el gozo del bien obrar, encontraba consuelos' (IV, ii; 138). There is a sense that Beatriz is schooling herself in a part, in which achievement and success are all-important: 'quiso apurar el sacrificio y adiestrarse en tan horrenda como eficaz escuela' (IV, ii; 138).

The fire of Nazarín's holiness also sparks a different fire — of anger — which will have its effect on Beatriz, as the chronicler somewhat mockingly notes: Pinto, infuriated at Beatriz's escapade, confronts her at the fountain of Méntrida/Aldea del Fresno: 'Pues ocurrió un hecho inesperado, de absoluta insignificancia en la vida total, mas para Beatriz de una gravedad extrema; uno de esos hechos

---

[13]Besides not endowing her with a confusing name, the chronicler refrains from applying numerous epithets. Only the enraged Pinto will proffer derogatory names: 'Mala cría', 'loca', 'grandísima puerca' (IV, iii; 144); 'infame, ruin pécora', 'putrefacción del mundo', 'tunanta', 'bribona' (V, iv; 200-01).

que en la vida individual equivalen a un cataclismo, diluvio, terremoto o fuego del Cielo. ¿Qué era? ... Nada, ¡que había visto al Pinto!' (IV, iii; 143). Her growing spirituality and works of charity, far from obliterating the memory of Pinto, only cause his physical reappearance 'para quitarle toda su cristiandad y precipitarla otravez en los abismos' (IV, iii; 143). Pinto's hold on Beatriz is not totally involuntary: she has been and continues to be strongly attracted by him, as her thoughts clearly reveal: 'El Pinto fue su amor y su tormento, el burlador de su honra, el estímulo de sus esperanzas, el que había despertado en su alma ensueños de ventura y despechos ardientes' (IV, iii; 143). Meritorious though her service in the villages has been, it is a sort of escape from the reality of her relationship with Pinto, which she must now squarely face and resolve.[14] The dilemma is not quite as Beatriz formulates it, for though it is true that Pinto would carry out his threat to kill them all if she does not join him at the inn next day to return to Madrid, she is surely misguided to think that Nazarín would not forgive her or welcome her back. For mistaken reasons — a fear of a future with Pinto as shameful as the past — Beatriz probably makes the right choice; the immediate consequence is that she is able to abort a nervous attack and tell the full story to Nazarín, who has guessed most of it from her facial expressions the previous night.

Her devotion to Nazarín grows to the point that she is prepared to take on his suffering in the approaching storm that both foresee. Her love is totally spiritual, she claims. Yet the dilution of the usual incendiary image with one of water suggests some sublimation of sexual feelings towards the priest:

> Beatriz sintió que en su alma se encendía súbitamente
> como una hoguera de cariño hacia el santo que las
> dirigía y las guiaba. Otras veces sintiera el mismo fuego,
> mas nunca tan intenso como en aquella ocasión.

[14]This temptation is represented 'como un rabillo de diablo [que] trazaba ondas de venenoso fuego por todo su ser' (IV, iii; 147). Later while they are cleaning the watering-hole (IV, v; 159), a non-poisonous snake climbs up one of Beatriz's legs. Panic is followed by laughter.

Después, observándose hasta lo más profundo, creyó que
no debía comparar aquel estado del alma al voraz
incendio que abrasa y destruye, sino a un raudal de agua
que milagrosamente brota de una peña y todo lo inunda.
Era un río lo que por su alma corría, y saliéndosele a la
boca, se derramaba fuera[...]. (IV, vi; 161)

Nazarín tries to control Beatriz's 'exaltación' by applying the image
of teacher and pupil, together with the traditional pastoral imagery:
'Hija mía, me quieres como a un maestro que sabe un poquito más
que tú y que te enseña lo que no sabes. Yo te quiero a ti, os quiero a
las dos, como el pastor a las ovejas, y si os perdéis os buscaré' (IV,
vi; 161). Beatriz is the over-enthusiastic pupil wanting to impress her
teacher. Significantly at the end of the conversation Beatriz will
innocently go to sleep on his shoulder, 'como un niño en el seno de
su madre' (IV, vi; 162). However, if the imagery slightly and
temporarily casts some criticism on her spiritual commitment, in her
final and supreme test — the march through her home town of
Móstoles — she will exhibit extreme fortitude and forbearance in the
face of great provocation from Pinto: she refrains from exchanging
verbal insults and plainly states her determination not to return to
him and then marches through Móstoles: 'con supremo tesón, sin
arrogancia, sin flaqueza, como quien apura un cáliz muy amargo,
pero en cuya amargura cree firmemente hallar la salud, arrostró el
doloroso tránsito, y creyó entrar en la Gloria cuando entraba en la
cárcel' (V, iv; 201).

   Notwithstanding Beatriz's moral courage, was this course of
action really necessary? Andara, like the Civil Guard Cirilo
Mondéjar, clearsightedly points out that, as she is not a prisoner, she
can leave the procession and rejoin them later. Beatriz's reasons for
rejecting this advice betray her unreasonable assurance about
Nazarín's reactions and her fear of hearing words of criticism from
her teacher. In the same conversation with Andara, Beatriz had tried
to outdo her companion in humility, claiming she was the worst
sinner, but without, like Andara, itemizing sins or suggesting that

she would have lived her life differently, if given a second chance. Beatriz believes that when she enters Móstoles jail she has reached Heaven. She also attains apotheosis in Nazarín's final battle visions where the Dantesque connotations of her name, as the epitorie of divine beauty, are fully realized. Yet the chronicler's exaggeratedly poetic style reduces this idealized status: 'Delante vio a Beatriz transfigurada. Su vulgar belleza era ya celeste hermosura, que en ninguna hermosura de la tierra hallaría su semejante, y un cerco de luz purísima rodeaba su rostro. Blancas como la leche eran sus manos, blancos sus pies, que andaban sobre las piedras como sobre nubes, y su vestidura resplandecía con suaves tintas de aurora' (V, vi; 206). Beatriz becomes as fanatical as Nazarín in the egotistical attainment of her ideal, ignoring surrounding reality and the feelings of her relations and friends in Móstoles: her comment to the Civil Guard, 'Cada uno a su religión' (IV, viii; 175), echoes that of Nazarín to Andara earlier when originally rejecting Beatriz's company: 'Cada cual con su conciencia, cada cual con su soledad' (III, iv; 96). Yet, on the other hand, the gains made by Beatriz, real and substantial, have to be balanced against these shortcomings. She has learnt to control her hysteria, she has severed all ties with Pinto, she has not returned to Madrid to become a prostitute, she has re-learnt some Catholic doctrine and is putting it into practice in her daily life. Like all the other characters, Beatriz is a bewildering amalgam of conflicting qualities.

Andara

Beatriz had been introduced by Andara almost half way through the text; Andara herself had enjoyed a longer exposure to the readers: as one of the group of 'tarascas' in Part I, her voice, albeit submerged in a chorus, had been effectively heard. In Part II she is given considerable prominence during her enforced stay in Nazarín's room. Like the priest's, her name can be a source of confusion. Its proper pronunciation will hinge upon the typographical incorporation (as in the Alianza edition) or omission of the accent on the first syllable. While an association — appropriate enough — with the verb of

motion, 'andar', is not suggested, a Biblical one is. Like the name
Nazarín, Andara is a contraction of Ana de Ara (II, ii; 45).[15] Like
Nazarín's, her identity at the window is not immediately
distinguishable and she is presented as a person of unshakable
conviction.[16] Nazarín is a saint and she is a sinner and this is 'la
realísima verdad', an opinion that loses some value when she admits
that in their previous encounter she had been the most insolent of the
group. All physical portraiture is omitted as Andara sketches her
own character through her own account of the incidents that have led
her to his room. In spite of her seriously weak condition, she proves
to be a masterful story-teller: 'yo estoy hablando, si me dejan, hasta
el día del *Perjuicio* final, y cuando me muera hablaré hasta un
poquito después de dar la última boqueada' (II, i; 43). She relates at
great length and with a liberal sprinkling of malapropisms ('*Perjuicio*
final') and oaths ('contra, mal ajo') amidst her brief, clipped
sentences, all the details of her fight with La Tiñosa.[17] The original
argument over a packet of pins had soon developed into a question
of honour: Andara cannot bear to hear words of public dishonour:
'Mira, padre, yo soy muy loba, tan loba como la primera, pero no

---

[15]Ara is the name of a river and a village in the province of Huesca, but it
also means 'altar'. Ana was, of course, the name of the mother of the Virgin
Mary. The Calle de Santa Ana is located very close to *Chanfaina*'s boarding-
house in Madrid: it is in this street that Andara purchases oil to start the fire.
According to Capmani, p.385, gypsy women had a special veneration for the
statue of Santa Ana found in the church of Santa María in this street. It is
also not without significance, in view of Andara's help to the plague-ridden
villages of Villamantilla and Villamanta, that during one great epidemic the
city of Madrid made special vows to this statue.

[16]There are other minor echoes of Part I: it is 'suerte' which allows the
fleeing Andara to slip into *Chanfaina*'s patio: the gypsies have left the
entrance door open, despite the late hour. It is also 'la voluble suerte', in the
form of *Chanfaina*, who will discover her after five days of hiding.

[17]The most memorable insult levelled at Andara is Pinto's phrase 'mujer más
fea que Tito' (IV, iii; 144). *Chanfaina* calls her 'mala sangre, hija de la gran
lobra, pelleja maldita' (II, iv; 56). Nazarín's friend, the 'cleriguito', refers to
her as a 'pelandusca', 'una criminal' (II, v; 65). The chronicler varies his
designation: 'la infame' (II, iii; 55), 'La temible amazona' (II, iv; 58), 'la
diabólica Andara' (II, iv; 56).

quiero que me lo digan' (II, i; 43).[18] In other words, Andara, as Beatriz will do later, does not want to hear the truth from others, even though she admits it to herself privately.

Andara vividly retells her tale and also re-creates the equally individualistic characters of her circle through her words; she uses colourful popular expressions which sometimes have unconscious ironic reverberations in the text: for example, when recounting the distant view of the flames springing from the roof of *Chanfaina*'s building, she uses pejorative expressions with a religious component: 'Por fin, ¡bendito Dios!, vio salir por encima de los tejados una columna de humo negro, más negro que el alma de Judas, y a los cielos subía retorciéndose con tremendos espirales, y creeríase que la humareda hablaba y que decía al par de ella: "¡Que aplique la *Camella* sus narices de perra pachona!... Anda, ¿no queríais tufo, señores caifases de la *incuria*?"' (II, iv; 59). 'El alma de Judas', 'caifases' are apt selections to express Andara's wicked glee at the hope of foiling the Law with this fire. But the association of these religious words with fire forms a counterpoint to the number of incendiary metaphors used to describe Beatriz's spiritual rebirth under Nazarín's guidance. Her humorous expression to describe unadulterated wine when giving Nazarín orders to buy a bottle ('y además, hay más conciencia que por aquí, vamos al decir, que no bautizan tanto', II, ii; 46) reminds the reader of *Chanfaina*'s baptismal certificate and the baptism of ,the Calle de las Amazonas on the first page of the text. At another point in this rambling report, Andara is able to link body and mind in a compelling way: 'De la conciencia, ¡mal ajo!, sentí que me corría la sangre, como de la herida' (II, i; 44). In both instances, the references to 'conciencia' inevitably call to mind Nazarín's frequent employment of the term. In Andara's case, the meaning is sincere and clear: she does have a real conscience in these moments of anguished remembrance, whereas Nazarín uses the word as an expedient, irrefutable cliché for

---

[18]The chronicler will again create ironic verbal echoes when, to describe the darkness of the night as Andara stealthily goes out of the building to buy the matches, he uses the popular expression: 'La calle estaba oscura como boca de lobo' (II, iv; 58).

his escape from the Law and the Church. Furthermore, it is Andara's true sense of conscience that leads her to commit the act of arson to save Nazarín from the police: 'Puede una ser una birria, pero tiene conciencia, y por conciencia no quiere una que al bueno le digan que es malo' (II, iv; 60).

After five days of forced confinement in Nazarín's room, Andara shows some signs of character development: no longer given to rambling accounts of her own misdeeds, she develops an interest in many aspects of life, asking Nazarín innumerable questions. The topics range from the sublime to the ridiculous: from the superstitions attached to the number two to a definition of the soul, in which her strikingly imaginative version contrasts favourably with Nazarín's rather abstract explanation:

> En toda ocasión la muerte es nuestra inseparable compañera y amiga. En nosotros mismos la llevamos desde el nacer, y los achaques, las miserias, la debilidad y el continuo sufrir son las caricias que nos hace dentro de nuestro ser.
>
> * * *
>
> — ¿De modo, padrito, que yo soy mi calavera? ¿Y el esqueleto mío es todos estos huesos, armados como los que vi yo una vez en el teatro, en la función de los fantoches? ¿Y cuando yo bailo, baila mi esqueleto? ¿Y cuando duermo, duerme mi esqueleto? ¡Mal ajo! ¿Y al morirme, cogen mi esqueletito salado y lo tiran a la tierra? (II, iii; 53)

When the two next meet - on the outskirts of Madrid, at the beginning of Part III - a very detailed physical portrait is given to highlight the change in Andara's physical appearance since her entrance into the novel as a heavily made-up 'tarasca' in Part I. Her basic ugliness is now clear for all to see: she is a dehumanized scarecrow whose body is 'todo ángulos' (III, i; 79), a certain reminder of the conglomeration of assorted structures and 'ángulos cortantes' in *Chanfaina's* patio. If Nazarín has trouble in recognizing her body, he is more surprised by the exceptional change in her demeanour: she is no longer the loquacious story-teller of their previous encounter, but is now tongue-tied and shy, 'con cierta cortedad infantil' (III, i; 79). The deterioration in her physical appearance contrasts, then, with the improvement in her demeanour and a desire to follow him to the ends of the earth, as she later confesses; the external and physical do not seem to count any more. However, one notable physical transformation seems to reflect this fundamental change of focus and direction in Andara's life: one eye is now more enlarged than the other. This optical infirmity, recalling that of the brandy seller outside *Chanfaina*'s portal, might imply that Andara's perspective on phenomenal reality has gone awry and that she can intuit greater spiritual truths, or it could suggest that her devotion to Nazarín is exaggerated and misdirected. The remainder of the text will provide limited help in resolving this uncertainty.

It would be inconsistent with the text's complexity to see in Beatriz and Andara a pair of complete opposites. It is true that Andara performs the more menial chores on the journey, like collecting wood and acorns, and that she is quicker to act, defending their possessions (against the two disguised bandits) or Nazarín (against arrest) or trying to help Nazarín escape from prison. But as the heroic deeds of Villamanta and Villamantilla demonstrate, she has to draw upon the reserves of her basic *amour propre* to overcome her sloth and distaste for the work, acting like a machine or a puppet (IV, ii; 137). Her *amour propre* will also bring her to complain that Nazarín loves Beatriz more than her (IV, vi; 162-63). Yet Beatriz's self-satisfaction at fulfilling her duty is not too far removed — perhaps at a different register — from Andara's basic self-concern: even the noblest of actions can be tainted by too much thought of one's self. And yet this analysis has also to be qualified in turn: though Andara is still propelled by 'dignidad' as in the initial fight with La Tiñosa, she is now channelling her physical energies to positive practical action; she does not react to provocation with physical vengeance and she listens to explanations and even apologizes, when, for instance, Ujo upbraids her for spitting at him in the arrest scene: 'Sería sin pensarlo, chiquitín del pueblo, mi coquito, mi *nanito* gracioso' (IV, viii; 175).

Andara does not really progress to any great spiritual summits, despite her dutiful saying of prayers and absorption of the catechism under Nazarín's teaching — she still wonders ingenuously at the relation of the beautiful night sky to the afterlife. Andara's real advances are in the fields of self-knowledge and self-correction, seen at their best and yet most fleeting in her night conversation with Beatriz in Navalcarnero prison. In this episode Andara reveals more common-sense realism than Beatriz, when urging her to bypass Móstoles or not to exaggerate her past sins. Andara's itemized account of her errors, uttered with genuine remorse, contrasts with Beatriz's emotional outburst: 'La verdad, ahora me pesa de todas las maldades y truhanerías que hice; pero como hemos de padecer tanto, porque así nos lo dice él, como no tenemos más remedio que aguantar y sufrir las crujías que vengan, yo no lloro, que tiempo habrá de llorar' (V, iii; 195).

Andara also has the moral strength to apologize for her earlier jealousy of Beatriz during their encampment in the castle and offers to take on Beatriz's sufferings herself because of her affection for her companion. And once more she sensibly tells Beatriz to stop crying, 'que las culpas feas que cometimos, yo más que tú, con estos trabajos y estas afrentas las estamos purgando' (V, iii; 195). Andara is no longer totally the impulsive performer of violent acts and words; she is now able to meditate and evaluate her past actions and see the differences between Beatriz and herself. But then Andara suddenly returns to more irrational ideas when acclaiming Nazarín's saintliness: 'a él le sacaría en volandas, diciendo: "Aquí está el que sabe la verdad de esta vida y la otra, el que no pecó nunca y tiene cuerpo y alma limpios como la patena, el santo nuestro y de todo el mundo cristiano y por cristianar"' (V, iii; 196). This profession of what is perceived as the truth has to be related to similar claims by other individuals in the novel. To say that Nazarín's only '*delincuencia*' is to console the poor, cure the sick and 'ser en todo un ángel de Dios y un serafín de la Virgen' is to ignore certain legalities and misrepresent the truth of what has happened so far in the book.

68 *Nazarín*

The arrest and unjust charges against Nazarín have turned Andara into a lioness and she is prepared to use violence to convince people of Nazarín's saintliness: 'la verdad con sangre entra[...] hay que dar algunos palos' (V, iii; 196). The pendulum of reason in this conversation now swings towards Beatriz for it is she who wisely reminds Andara of the sixth commandment, 'Thou shalt do no murder'. However the pendulum soon swings back to Andara when she retorts that evil can be opposed by force as well as by prayers and that the Catholic Church has many warrior saints like St Michael, St Paul and St Ferdinand. The militant and the pietist may be opposing tendencies, but they can and do coexist, as Andara reasons: 'Beatriz, tú tienes culpas; yo también. Cada una las lava como sabe y como puede, según su natural... Tú, con lágrimas; yo ..., ¡qué sé yo!' (V, iii; 197). The coexistence of opposites, if not their reconciliation, is a reality that is not recognized or accepted by people who insist on their own univisional interpretation of truth. It is thus an ideal not achieved in normal society. As if to signpost this conclusion, the chronicler terminates the chapter as he had the previous one, recounting the conversation of *El Sacrílego* and Nazarín after the latter's beating in the men's cell, by referring — in almost the same words — to the arrival of dawn: 'Cuando esto decían se asomó a las altas rejas la claridad del alba' (V, iii; 197) ('Cuando esto decían, penetraba por las altas rejas la luz del alba', V, ii; 193). The atmospheric change is surely a visual shorthand to confirm this inevitable coexistence of opposites: as day succeeds night so the militancy of Andara will be followed by the more tranquil Christianity of Beatriz, just as the drubbing of Nazarín is followed by the conversion of *El Sacrílego*.

Andara and Beatriz have a close and symbiotic relationship with each other and with their master. A very serious threat to this triangle is that represented by the contacts of both women with two other men, who in turn form another contrast mirroring that of Andara and Beatriz. Again, as if to confuse our narrative focus, these two characters, who should, because of their relatively brief appearances, be regarded as minor characters, are accorded considerable importance because of the effects of their words on the trio and their potential involvement in the unfolding of the plot.

Pinto

As with the names of other characters, a certain confusion surrounds the correct form of Pinto's, it is either Pinto or Pintón, Andara, half uncertain, says (III, iv; 96). The man's attitude to Beatriz is at one time scornful, at another cajoling. Whilst this preliminary information from Andara to Nazarín suggests that he is still interested in Beatriz, his eventual confrontation with her at the fountain of the square in Méntrida/Aldea del Fresno comes as a surprise both to Beatriz and the reader. With his ultimatum, that Beatriz should meet him next day at the local inn in order to return to Madrid, he constitutes a serious disruption to Nazarín's travels as well as to the plot of the novel. But, of course, this potentially abrupt change of direction is aborted when — rather comically — he is forced to desist from the night attack on the castle by the sudden emergence of a fog. (Pinto has another chance to disrupt the plot when he once more tries to dissuade Beatriz from entering Móstoles; however, this option is really illusory, because the Civil Guards conducting the party would prevent such action.) Their encounter, reproduced in a flashback by Beatriz as she returns to the castle, discloses Pinto's impetuous character, his strong language, with the occasional solecism and oath, and his handsome figure, which obviously still attracts Beatriz. And yet his concern about the public shame Beatriz will suffer if she continues in Nazarín's company is sincerely felt and not to be summarily dismissed: he does not abduct her on the spot, but gives her the chance to reconsider the matter (IV, iii; 144-45). Pinto's energetic but primitive defence of conventional social codes of honour does not allow any consideration, of the nature of Beatriz's newly-found spiritual values. Yet in the frustration of his attempts to maintain the traditional male honour code, Pinto becomes a figure of fun, reduced to helplessness. This development is also reflected linguistically: in the fountain encounter he had arrogantly assured Beatriz: 'Ya sabes que yo

cuando digo lo que digo, lo digo ... diciéndolo; quiere decirse, como
el que sabe hacer lo que dice' (IV, iii; 145). Pinto's almost Freudian
slip of the tongue really does anticipate his final comical situation.
His words of bravado remain only words of bravado: he cannot
follow them with actions. Thus, he exclaims at the outskirts of
Móstoles 'Lo veo y no lo creo' (V, iv; 200). The reasons for this
inaction are not merely circumstantial: Beatriz's own inner
conviction of her new life is the ultimate deterrent against her
abduction.

Ujo

Conforming to the text's basically confusing perspectives, the picture
of the dwarf's body, the most extensive portrait in the novel, is
disproportionate to his actual physical size as well as to the brevity
of his appearances. Ujo is the ugliest, most deformed and ridiculous
dwarf imaginable:

> La primera impresión que producía el verle era la de una
> cabeza que andaba por sí, moviendo dos piececillos
> debajo de la barba. Por los costados de un capisayo
> verde que gastaba, semejante a las fundas que cubren las
> jaulas de machos de perdiz, salían dos bracitos de una
> pequeñez increíble. En cambio, la cabeza era más
> voluminosa de lo regular, feísima, con una trompa por
> nariz, dos alpargatas por orejas, unos pelos lacios en
> bigote y barba y ojuelos de ratón que miraban el uno
> para el otro, porque bizcaban horriblemente. (IV, iv;
> 152)

The immediate purpose of this description is clearly to form a
contrast with Pinto's handsome figure, which also reflects the
corresponding contrast of physical appearance between their respective amours. Yet Ujo also serves as a contrast to Nazarín in his status
as a beggar: he does not wander the roads looking for new hardships:
he is always in the village street or the houses of the rich and poor

looking for scraps of food and rags of clothes. He is simply a beggar without Nazarín's pompous preaching. For his earnings he has to endure all sorts of taunts and malicious jokes: 'era objeto de chacota y befa[...] los chicos del pueblo tenían con él un Carnaval continuo' (IV, iv; 152). Ujo is a warning of what is soon to befall the priest in greater measure. A few small points increase the analogy with Nazarín: Ujo's name is as much a verbal enigma as Nazarín's: 'Le llamaban *Ujo*, palabra que no se sabe si era nombre o apellido o las dos cosas juntas' (IV, iv; 152).[19] If Nazarín's figure suggests that of a woman, Ujo's voice is that of a child, yet his language is uncouth and malicious. Nazarín had received from the Peludos an old cloak or blanket for sole vestment; Ujo wears a green cape similar to the green baize used to cover bird cages. At the castle, Ujo will sport a soldier's cap, which, as well as reminding us of the soldiers on manoeuvres in Part III, anticipates the medieval battle of Nazarín's vision, and in particular Andara's shining helmet similar to that of St Michael. During his stay at the castle of Méntrida/Aldea del Fresno, Nazarín will also sport headgear: the handkerchiefs his two female followers bind around his wounded head form a turban.

Ujo is a permanent fixture of the village: 'era como parte integrante del pueblo mismo, como la veleta de la torre, o el escudo del Ayuntamiento, o el mascarón del caño de la fuente. No hay función sin tarasca, ni aldea sin Ujo' (IV, iv; 153). The reader is inevitably reminded by the words 'tarasca' and 'mascarón' of the events of Part I: Ujo is a permanent Carnival figure, however, whose physical features are completely abnormal and disproportionate. Like the brandy-seller at *Chanfaina*'s boarding-house and Andara, he is squint-eyed, an optical infirmity that suggests that Ujo may have an abnormal, but also perhaps privileged and intuitive, attitude to life. Indeed, the chronicler highlights, in suitably confusing syntax, this contradiction: the most grotesque physical body contains the most Christian soul to be found in the book: 'Parecía que no, pero era un buen hombre, mejor dicho, un buen enano o un buen monstruo, el

---

[19]Ujo is also the name of a village in Asturias. He is called '*nano*', 'nanito', 'Ujito' (IV, v; 156-57) by Andara, and 'el gran Ujo' by the chronicler (IV, viii; 173).

pobre Ujo' (IV, iv; 153). The food, especially fruit delicacies, that
Ujo earns at the price of so much humiliating jesting is given to
Beatriz and Andara out of genuine kindness. But more helpful are
his warnings about the impending visits of Pinto and the mayor to
the castle and the rumours circulating about the trio which he knows
are lies. He is a messenger and the repetition of the archaic 'diz'
shows to what use he applies his speech, the most vivid and
colourful in the novel, even surpassing that of the old gypsy (in Part
I), in solecisms, oaths, fragmented syntax and staccato style.

Ujo takes refuge from the constant abuse of villagers in the
local church (we see Nazarín only once in a church setting, and then
only from the outside — when he spends the day in the temple of
Móstoles after seeing the sick daughter of Fabiana). Ujo is so
integrated into the church of Méntrida/Aldea del Fresno that, to
Beatriz, he appears a devil bouncing out of one of the altarpieces
depicting 'las Animas benditas' (IV, iv; 153) — ironically Pinto had
called Beatriz at their fountain meeting 'un ánima del Purgatorio'(IV,
iii; 144).

Ujo's spontaneously sincere declaration of love for Andara is
also made in the setting of the village church, but it is not without its
comic side, just as Pinto's admission to Beatriz at the fountain also
had its serious tone. However, there is a difference of linguistic
registers: while Pinto says 'te quiero', Ujo remarks more politely: 'te
estimo'. Ujo's love for Andara is so generous that it ignores passing
verbal and physical insults. He is even prepared to fight God to
defend her — appropriately here identified as 'la *Verba* divina'(IV,
viii; 175). Yet this genuine love for Andara, despite all her faults, is
also Ujo's contradiction, for he believes unrealistically that he can
persuade Andara to leave Nazarín and stay with him, just as Pinto
urges Beatriz to do. Given Andara's status as a member of the chain
gang and a wanted criminal, Ujo's expectations are pathetically
unrealistic: he is obliged to watch her leave town: 'Al frente de los
curiosos se veía la cabeza oscilante de Ujo, el cual fue dando convoy
a la estimada de su corazón hasta donde la debilidad de sus cortas
piernas se lo permitía. Cuando tuvo que quedarse atrás, se le vio
arrimado a un árbol, con la mano en los ojos' (IV, viii; 178). His legs

will not be able to take him away from Méntrida/Aldea del Fresno, nor will Andara's feet want to stop following Nazarín. Ujo ignores these realities.

d) Minor Characters with a Purpose

For a novel that on the one hand hardly ever allows its eponymous hero to leave centre stage and that on the other has a short cast of secondary characters (six), *Nazarín* contains a large number of walk-on characters. Their presence in Part I, where they number thirty-two, can be explained by the selection of a locale that is commonly associated with the constant coming and going of a large number of people. In Parts II to V Nazarín, forced to abandon this fixed location (6, p.213), chooses to embark on a peripatetic way of life that by its very nature and purpose also involves his frequent and brief acquaintance with a host of characters (twenty-four in Part II, twenty-two in Part III, thirty in Part IV and seventeen in Part V, excluding unnumbered groups of people). A consequence of this type of open-ended narration, proper to medieval romances of chivalry and the picaresque novel, is that many of these minor figures might merely be narrative ballast mentioned in passing by the secondary characters or the chronicler, as is the case with La Roma in Part II or some of the Villamantilla plague victims in Part IV. However, Galdós's achievement in *Nazarín* is to ensure that a surprisingly large number of these characters contribute to the greater elucidation of the pattern of confusing images that is the novel's essential texture.

Part II

The sudden and complete separation which the narrator would have us believe exists between Part I and the rest of *Nazarín* is really an illusion, for just as there is no change of locale in the first few pages of the new chronicle, so old characters reappear: *Chanfaina* is there once more to forward the action, but in a surprising sort of way. Her hammering on Nazarín's window shutters will indeed initiate the

priest's departure from the boarding-house and eventually lead to his
sally into the Castilian countryside. But this is not the result
Chanfaina is expecting or planning at this momen⁺ when her
immediate aim is to remove Andara from Nazarín's room.

The reader also has to revise initial impressions of the
landlady's frequent use of popular words and phrases. It is true that
many of those directed to Andara are expressions of violent abuse;
but others, like the duly italicized malapropism 'interfezta', the
solecism 'espital' (II, iv; 55) or familiar phrase 'cuando les pica una
pulga', create a more comic effect, while such modes of address as
'Señor Nazarillo de mis pecados' or '*San Cándido*' reveal that 'la
hombruna patrona', 'la terrible amazona' (II, iv; 57-58) is capable of
tenderness to others.

However, *Chanfa* is more than the articulator of colourful
expressions: she is also a very effective performer of generous
actions as when first she fetches fresh clothes for Andara and then
rushes off to prepare a meal for her lodgers. In fact, it is this
generosity of spirit that will accelerate the advance of the plot in Part
II: *Chanfa* readily permits Andara to fetch the water with which to
clean the room and then gives her some money to buy drink and
cigarettes. The prostitute rushes off, however, to buy some matches
with which she sets light to the whole house. *Chanfa*'s generosity
leads, then, paradoxically, to her own loss and suffering. Yet this
interpretation has to be qualified by the following considerations.
First, when she declares unequivocally to Andara's face that she
never believes a word the prostitute says ('¿Miento yo alguna vez?
— Alguna vez, no; siempre', II, iv; 58), the reader is entitled to
question *Chanfa*'s motives for handing the coin to Andara. Is her
generosity an involuntary act of foolishness that contradicts her
appreciation of Andara's character, or does she have some inkling of
what the woman might do with the money? Some confirmation of
this second possibility emerges, again indirectly, from the landlady's
own comments to Nazarín as she protects her possessions from
robbery in the street while the fire rages. So far we have been led to
believe that *Chanfa* is the owner of her own establishment, as when
she observes: 'los pudientes[...] tenemos que sacar los trastos a la

calle' (II, v; 62). However, the 'ajuar' she has rescued with such frenetic action from the flames is fit only for scrapwood, according to the chronicler. Then *Chanfa* herself reveals that there is a certain 'amo de la casa' whom she refrains from identifying by name. In an even more astounding statement she reveals that he will be delighted to hear of the house's destruction, as the insurance company will have to reimburse the costs of replacing the building whose real value is practically nothing. So the Great Fire of the Calle de las Amazonas is not really a disaster for its owner, as it first appeared. Perhaps *Chanfa* herself will not be too inconvenienced in the long run, for despite the suitably incendiary language she directs to the insouciant Nazarín ('Sí, pavito de Dios, ¡mala centella nos parta a todos!', II, v; 62), the reader is entitled to surmise that the landlord will soon install her in a new boarding-house. The more *Chanfa* speaks, the more she reveals herself to be a complex character. The final layer of surprise that effectively inserts this singular woman into the fabric of linguistic paradoxes or ambiguities is unveiled when she reminds Nazarín that if there is no insurance money forthcoming, then some embarrassing, finger-pointing comments might appear in the 'papeles' (II, v; 63). *Chanfa*, that great employer of speech, now pays due homage to the more permanent and lasting power of the printed word, especially of a legal nature (and we should not forget her close contacts with that court-hanger-on, Blas Portela).

Other characters to reappear from Part I include Andara's three fellow prostitutes, but their re-entry into the *History of Nazarín* is distanced through the evocative reminiscences of Andara herself. Surprisingly, however, they are given far more vivid portraits than those sketched for others by the chronicler. For example, La Tiñosa, Andara's adversary, has 'ojos de carnero a medio morir, el labio partido, la oreja rajada, de un tirón que le dieron para arrancarle el pendiente, y la garganta llena de costurones' (II, i; 42). Of more endearing memory for Andara is the unnamed street-cleaner who would send her dirty camelias he had picked up at the doors of theatres or mansions on Shrove Tuesday. This little anecdote not only refers us back to the Carnivalesque goings-on in Part I, but also

reminds us that one of Andara's former acquaintances, appropriately
nicknamed *Camellas*, a corruption of the phrase 'la dama de las
camelias' taken from Alexandre Dumas's novel, had almost
discovered her whereabouts earlier in the day when sniffing at the
window. If this single word can forge sudden and surprising associ-
ations between disparate events, the reminiscence itself shows that
Andara, like *Chanfa*, is capable of feeling affection for others as well
as arousing affection in them for her, despite the violence of her
language. What would otherwise appear as a parody of a common
Romantic motif is spared this interpretation by the sincerity of
feelings of the two people involved. In contrast, Nazarín's sarcastic
reaction, '¡Qué fino!', and subsequent injunction to forget such
'tonterías' and concentrate on saving her soul (II, iii; 52), disclose a
surprising lack of perception and sensitivity on his part.

Another anecdote from Andara elicits a similarly petulant
response from the priest. Again, she details the etymology of her
friend's nickname: 'de una canción muy chusca que acababa siempre
con el estribillo de *el bálsamo del amor* le vino y se le quedó para
siempre el nombre de *Bálsamo*' (II, ii; 48). The interest of this
recollection lies not in *Bálsamo*'s physical appearance or actions but
in his career history. When young, he had been first a verger then a
candidate for the priesthood before blindness forced him to sing for a
living in the streets. Furthermore, *Bálsamo*, like *El Tripita*, had tried
to convince Andara that the existence of a Purgatory or Hell was
utter nonsense. At a time when Nazarín is trying to inculcate the
notion of Christian repentance, Andara's oral reminiscence of this
ex-candidate for the priesthood is powerful enough to provoke a
testy response from the ordained priest: 'Pues escoge entre la opinión
del señor de *Bálsamo* y la mía' (II, ii; 48).

Bálsamo, who seems to renounce the religious connotations of
his nickname, is, in fact, one of a series of clerical or quasi-clerical
figures to appear in Part II, just as Nazarín is preparing to abandon
the priesthood. The next figure in this series is the parish priest of
San Cayetano whose surname is Rubín. All that the chronicler tells
us is that he has summoned Nazarín for a meeting after novena one
day. For the cognoscenti of Galdós's work there is additional hidden

significance in this name, for if the priest is the same Nicolás Rubín who had been presented so vividly in *Fortunata y Jacinta* as a crassly ambitious yet completely ineffectual spiritual adviser to Fortunata, then Nazarín's planned meeting with him might not be a success. This is all pure conjecture, of course, but Galdós, who was never averse from playing literary jokes on his regular readers, could have selected this name precisely to trigger a whole series of intriguing and bewildering literary echoes.

To another priest, the 'cleriguito', is given the task of advancing the plot even further. At the same time he contributes his own small measure of confusion to the general pattern of the novel. At first he appears a genuine friend, attending to Nazarín's every need, even making him a present of a breviary. When Nazarín is summoned to court to make a statement in the case against Andara, his colleague expresses all the reservations and concern that a good friend might be expected to make. But the chronicler now adds some new and disturbing judgements on the young priest. He no longer refers to him as 'el amigo' or 'el joven sacerdote' but as 'el dichoso cleriguito' who is also very 'entrometido y oficioso' when it comes to other people's business (II, v; 64), and likes to pull strings with his well-placed contacts in the Madrid Establishment. So what initially appeared as a disinterested and friendly concern gradually develops into an opportunity for great self-satisfaction and social pride. His snobbery and smugness are very much in evidence when he reports the outcome of his visit to the Judge in relation to Nazarín's involvement: 'por la noche tuvo la indecible satisfacción de espetar a don Nazario el siguiente discurso' (II, v; 64). By skilfully reserving the use of direct speech for this point in Nazarín's stay at his friend's house, Galdós is able to let the young cleric reveal his true character through his own words. Indeed this is no conversation between two friends, but a pompous speech from a snob to an acquaintance he no longer wishes to have in his house. But even here, the decision does not seem to be that of 'el cleriguito' but of his possessive mother. Again it is words and their possible ambiguities that determine shifts in the action: 'Pero lo que dice mamá: "Basta que suenen las hablillas, aun siendo injustas, para que no podamos tener a ese bendito en casa..."' (II, v; 66).

The speech of the 'cleriguito', worthy of characters destined to play greater roles in the novel, is a veritable linguistic tour de force. It is a farrago of all sorts of rhetorical devices which, in their chaotic juxtaposition, create very comic effects. Latin phrases are used either to avoid the normal Castilian designation for someone unpleasant (a prostitute): 'con ésa y otras *ejusdem fúrfuris*' (II, v; 65), or to impress his attentive listener with excessive (and therefore insincere) flattery: 'Y finalmente, mi querido Nazario, ya sabe que somos amigos, *ex toto corde*, que le tengo a usted por hombre impecable, por hombre puro, *pulchérrimo viro*' (II, v; 65-66). And yet he is also capable of going to the other extreme of the linguistic register: '¿En qué demonios pensaba usted al recibir en su domicilio a una pelandusca semejante, a una criminal, a una...?' (II, v; 65). In some sentences the two opposing levels of speech come together in incongruous juxtaposition: 'Usted es incapaz..., y si se dejara tentar por el demonio de la concupiscencia, lo haría sin duda, con *féminas* de mejor pelaje' (II, v; 65). The same contrast is evident in his choice of syntax: on the one hand, there are such familiar exclamative phrases as '¡Qué bochorno, amigo querido! Bien sé que es mentira. ¡Si nos conocemos!' (II, v; 65); on the other, long, involved, symmetrically-structured clauses full of abstract nouns: 'Fácil es a sus calumniadores deshonrarle; difícil, dificilísimo le será a usted destruir el error; que la maledicencia encuentra calor en todos los corazones, transmisión en todas las bocas, mientras que la justificación nadie la cree, nadie la propaga' (II, v; 65). Yet, in both instances, the effect is the same: the reader begins to doubt the speaker's sincerity because of the studied repetition or accumulation. The exaggerated rhetoric seems to signal a discrepancy between the reality of Nazarín's situation and the priest's distorted imagination of it. That his rhetoric and its falsely imagined base dictate his behaviour is clearly proved when, after he has referred to 'asuntos viles, cuya sola mención pone los pelos de punta' (II, v; 65), the chronicler reports that the hair of the 'cleriguito' does almost stand on end 'de terror y vergüenza' (II, v; 65). For the young priest words become the means by which he can still present himself, at least on the surface, which is where it matters, as a friend to Nazarín. Yet his choice of words and his syntax betray at the same time (to attentive readers, even if not to the listener Nazarín) his real feelings of scorn and repulsion for the latter's misdemeanour. At the start of his 'discurso' he had declared: 'Mire usted, compañero, cuanto más amigos más claros' (II, v; 64). Yet the rest of the speech with its double level of meaning exposes the hollowness of this claim, so that when at the end he assures Nazarín, 'No es esto echarle, compañero' (II, v; 66), he is speaking the truth — after all, he has not told Nazarín to leave the house — , and at the same time a lie — for he and his mother really do want their guest to leave.

Verbal ambiguity or equivocation is also present in the approach of the 'cleriguito' to what will become one of the central questions of the novel: Nazarín's madness: 'Pues el juez, que es todo un caballero, lo primero que me preguntó fue si usted está loco. Respondíle que no sabía... No me atreví a negarlo, pues siendo usted cuerdo, resulta más inexplicable su conducta' (II, v; 65). Here, irony of ironies, the young priest's use of a series of negative clauses, one the contradiction of the other, captures exactly the real perplexity experienced by himself and others when confronted by this question. Here, indeed, confusing verbal expressions are not meant primarily to bewilder the listener, but rather reflect the confused state of mind of the speaker.

The ultimate irony of the 'cleriguito's speech is that, in throwing Nazarín out of his house, albeit ever so politely, he, as a fellow representative of Christ, is also expelling himself and thereby contributing to the re-enactment of the paradigmatic life-story of Christ that Nazarín will relive in greater detail at the end of the chronicle. Here again, the deeper meaning of some casual popular expressions uttered by the 'cleriguito' foreshadow this development in a way that no one can fully appreciate at this point in a first reading: 'El mundo es muy malo, la Humanidad, inicua, traidora, y no hace más que pedir eternamente que le suelten a Barrabás y que crucifiquen a Jesús[...] prepárese para que le traigan y le lleven de Herodes a Pilatos, tomándole declaraciones' (II, v; 65).

Reservations of another kind can be applied to the charity shown Nazarín by the elderly couple, Los Peludos, to whom he repairs after his ejection from the 'cleriguito's house. The chronicler informs us that they are 'gente pobre, y suplía el lujo con la buena voluntad' (II, vi; 67), a judgement that does not seem to accord with the details given earlier about their long-established hardware business, when the chronicler had pertinently mentioned 1850 as its date of foundation. Furthermore, our first impressions about the couple's generosity undergo some revision: Nazarín had hoped to repay their hospitality with money from saying masses in nearby churches, but when these are not forthcoming, he offers to take any job in order to repay his hosts. The husband is scandalized by the idea, frightened at what Church and Society might say. The wife, on the other hand, supports the idea, even offering to look out for a suitable job and boarding-house. But behind this proposal lies a more selfish concern — that Nazarín leave their house as soon as possible — as the chronicler openly comments: 'a lo que contestaron ambos disuadiéndole de salir a correr aventuras, él con verdadera sinceridad y calor, ella con medias palabras, sin duda porque deseaba verle marchar con viento fresco' (II, vi; 71). They provide him with old pieces of clothing, and pack his travelling bag with plenty of food. Nevertheless, this charity smacks of a certain degree of smugness and self-satisfaction: 'dijéronle que no se afanase por el pago de la corta deuda, pues ellos, *como gente muy cristiana y con su poquito de santidad en el cuerpo* [my italics], le hacían donación del *comestible* devengado' (II, vi; 71). The use of other pretentious locutions by the couple ('Lo *cual* que', '*quedar a deberles*', '*a la que estamos*', '*consumo*', II, vi; 71) reinforces this impression. Finally, the chronicler's stuffy designation of them as 'honrados bienhechores' perhaps captures correctly this touch of officiousness in what had appeared initially as totally sincere charity.

With the last minor character of Part II, the theme of deceptive appearances is given a new twist. Even the humorous appelation by which he goes, Paco Pardo, is not his proper name but the invention of others; the second designation used, 'el hijo de la Canóniga', throws no light on his real name either. The mystery of his character as he approaches Nazarín one morning on the city outskirts is deepened by his physical appearance. For a character who will be present in the novel only for a brief while the details of his features are numerous: he is 'un hombre muy mal encarado, flaco de cuerpo, cetrino de rostro, condecorado con más de una cicatriz, vestido pobremente' (II, vi; 69). The justification of this detailed description soon becomes apparent: his intimidating physical features suggest that he could be a smuggler or a horse-dealer, but his exceptionally polite mode of address to Nazarín seems more proper to someone from a higher social class. In fact, in all his experience as a priest, Nazarín has never been addressed with such respect. The chronicler underlines the exceptional nature of this occurrence by adding parenthetically: 'Y respetuosamente, así como suena' (II, vi; 69), and then by giving Pardo an appropriate 'muletilla': 'con respeto'. This is another instance of a verbal cliché ironically possessing all of its original meaning simply because the speaker is not using it as a rhetorical device.

Part III

Like *Chanfaina*, Paco Pardo straddles two successive Parts. His second and final appearance, so soon after the first (one day later), is used to underline the artificiality of the change in Nazarín's external appearance, now that of an anchorite. In spite of his insistent staring, Paco is able to recognize the priest only through his voice. In turn, though with less justification, Nazarín fails to recognize Paco, and even to remember the details of their conversation the previous day (which he wrongly places further back in the past). The reasons for this apparent error become clear, however, when Paco reports that Andara is in the vicinity picking wild flowers: Nazarín, in his immediate desire to disappear over the horizon, shows that he is trying desperately to forget his past life and acquaintances, even if this means being rude and unfriendly to those like Paco and Andara who merely want to help him.

Nazarín's new artificial figure had already, in fact, been called into question the moment he walked across the Puente de Toledo to start his journey, when a group of beggars stared with suspicion and in surprise at the newcomer to the profession. But now it is the turn of Nazarín himself to be confronted by audio-visual enigmas. First, the soldiers he sees moving across country and firing their guns are not involved in a real battle but merely on manoeuvres in this army training area. Significantly, it is the eyes of his first follower, a lean hungry dog he had met on the Camino de Carabanchel Bajo, which confirm this corrected interpretation as well as pointing out the generosity of soldiers at meal times, as he gazes up at his new master. Some of the phrases the chronicler inserts into this visual message, such as 'esto es todo de mentirijillas[...] aquel lindo juego' (III, ii; 81) are reminiscent of the ludic elements mentioned in Part I. But, as on that occasion, so now the humour of the chronicler's words is not able to fully conceal a message of some seriousness for the new direction on which Nazarín is embarking. Just as he is on the point of abandoning the order of civilized Spanish society and entering what he imagines to be a brave new world of total personal freedom, he is confronted by the ultimate defenders of the former. A clear enough warning, one would have thought, for Nazarín to rethink his plans for a new life.

A more precise focus is given to this warning by the next person he encounters on the country road: a goatherd, who, despite his 'ladino' appearance and actions (he scrounges some bread off Nazarín, and would have taken some wine if there had been any available), is kind enough to inform Nazarín that the Civil Guards have been given orders to round up all vagrants and return them to Madrid. Using frequent popular forms ('*paíce*', '*anduviéis*', '*ceviles*', '*palante*', '*mantención*', '*seis*', '*recogimientos*', III, ii; 81-82), the goatherd remarks that the prisoners are often freed once they get to Madrid because of the overcrowding in prisons. Once again, our priest gives no indication that he is able to interpret and ponder these visual and oral warnings, simply because, one feels, he does not believe that what is happening in the world around him has any relevance for the new kind of life he wishes to lead.

Having strategically introduced these warnings, the chronicler now moves on to a different group of minor characters — those who will confront Nazarín with conflicting examples of human behaviour. At first, after being given vegetables by two peasant women and a boy and then a coin by three men whom he helps to move a cart from a rut, Nazarín firmly believes that his first few experiences have been blessed with good fortune. He soon discovers, however, that people can be both rude of word and cruel of action, as when he is driven in no uncertain terms from a farmyard by a red-faced, well-dressed owner who is determined not to shelter any more robbers on his property. Words and actions here are crystal clear for the listener, yet the initial premise of the speaker — that Nazarín is a thief like all beggars — is obviously an error.

A slightly less inhospitable welcome is accorded him by three fellow beggars preparing a stew in a tumbledown shack close to the farm. They readily accept Nazarín's offer of bread, yet selfishly announce that they are unable to give him any of their stew because they are more 'pobres que el que inventó la pobreza' (III, ii; 84) and leave him the roughest sleeping area. Surely, though, of greater relevance in this episode is the beggars' question about the economic situation in the capital, which Nazarín dismisses simply because of his lack of interest in the matter, thereby failing to appreciate the influence of socio-economic factors on people's behaviour.[20]

La Polonia, a friend of Beatriz, whom the wandering trio meet after Nazarín has returned from Belmonte's mansion, is another minor character who is a cause for some reflection. It is certainly true that she confirms for the most part Nazarín's impressions of 'el señor de la Coreja' and then helps in the distribution of Nazarín's hamper of food from Belmonte to the poor and needy of Sevilla La Nueva, finally directing the trio to the plague-infested village of Villamantilla. Nazarín is grateful for the help and guidance, but he fails to ponder Polonia's circumstances; for instance, if she is a small

---

[20]See El Imparcial (9 February 1895) for the desperate plight of the unemployed in Andalusia. Rabanal Taylor (54) refers to 1895 as a year of socio-economic crisis in Spain. The topographical details of this region were in all likelihood culled from Pascual Madoz, Diccionario geográfico-estadístico-histórico de España y sus posesiones de Ultramar (Madrid: 1845- 50), vols I, II, XI-XIV, XVI.

landowner to some extent — she owns a turnip field — , how has she not given some of her own produce to the people of Sevilla la Nueva ('Pueblo más mísero y pobre no le hay por acá', III, ix; 126)? Moreover, she shows that she has an extensive knowledge of Belmonte's past life. Could she, in fact, have been one of his mistresses who has now been bought off with a small plot of land? If so, her account of Belmonte's character could be correspondingly distorted. Nazarín, however, gives no indication that he has thought of any of these questions.

Part IV

We noted earlier that in Part II there is a cluster of minor clerical figures positioned around Nazarín as he makes his decision to abandon the priesthood. Now, in Part IV, Galdós introduces a series of contrasting 'alcalde' figures.[21] The most prominent is the garrulous mayor of Méntrida/Aldea del Fresno who conducts the final interrogation of Nazarín, but there is also the hard-pressed figure of the mayor of Villamantilla. Paradoxically, his 'arenga de bienvenida' turns out to be an order for Nazarín and his followers to abandon the village. But his mistake is completely understandable in the situation in which the emaciated mayor and the small band of survivors find themselves. With his touch of 'pundonor', like Calderón's Alcalde de Zalamea ('Soy el alcalde, y lo que digo digo', IV, i; 136), he is the

---

[21]It is perhaps noteworthy that Galdós did not include the Mayor of Móstoles or even his title amongst this group of local government officials —— he does present, however, the secretary of Móstoles's town council. For, undoubtedly, there would have been some ironic reverberations, as a famous historical predecessor, Don Juan Pérez de Villaamil, during the War of Spanish Independence, issued a public notice calling upon the rest of the country to aid Madrid after the bloody events of 2 May 1808. Galdós had recalled the details of this episode in an 1874 newspaper article: see Leo J. Hoar Jr., 'More on the Pre-(and Post-) History of the *Episodios Nacionales*. Galdós' Article "El Dos de Mayo" (1874)', *AG*, 8 (1973), 107-20, especially p.115 and p.120 (note 23). There is also a series of judges in the novel: the judge who takes Nazarín's statement(II, v; 64) might or might not be 'el juez de la Inclusa' who issues the arrest warrant (IV, vii; 167). The mayor of Méntrida/Aldea del Fresno is advised by 'un juez municipal' (IV, viii; 176).

exemplary leader, attending to the comfort of the sick and the burial of the dead. Words and deeds need not necessarily be the causes of constant mystification as they were in Part I, recalled here by references to such victims of the plague as a prostitute and a formerly handsome youth who now has a 'máscara horrible que ocultaba su rostro' (IV, ii; 139). In Villamantilla, the more sombre and tragic implications of the Shrove Tuesday events in Madrid are given prominence. Carnaval is not always synonymous with the pleasantly ludic or comic; it is indeed inseparable from death and suffering.

Nazarín is again confronted by a series of contrasting experiences. Though some people ploughing a field offer him bread, vegetables, and money, those tending vines on a river bank, who initially seem well-off and pleasant, eventually drive him and his two followers away because of the superstitious fears of some of the female labourers. Yet the dismissal is not quite the 'cruel despedida' (IV, v; 158) the chronicler says that it is, for the labourer who had killed three rabbits with his gun presents one and a coin to the party before they leave. More money is the reward for the hard work of Nazarín and Andara in helping some men clean a cattle watering-place. Generosity and cruelty succeed one another with regularity, offering a corrective to Nazarín's unidimensional view that life in general and his odyssey in particular have to be a series of misfortunes and nothing else.

Nazarín's eventual capture by the mayor of Méntrida/Aldea del Fresno is grotesquely foreshadowed by the vicious assault carried out on him by El Sacrílego and El Parricida who pretend to be undercover Civil Guards acting on Government orders to recover stolen goods, though not to apprehend the malefactors. The whole episode, according to the chronicler, is the work of a 'terrible humorista', it is a 'broma' which ends with 'la estúpida diversión' (IV, v; 159) of the stoning of the defenceless trio. Unlike the Villamantilla stoning, this incident combines in one both aspects of the Carnaval image established in Part I: the practical joke-playing together with the personal physical suffering of individuals.

Part V

The bogus Civil Guards reappear as members of the chain gang
being marched back to Madrid. If the animalistic, swarthy, *El
Parricida* will remain unrepentant of his physical and verbal abuse
of Nazarín, so aptly misrepresented by the criminal to the Civil
Guards as a 'broma' (V, ii; 191), his ex-partner undergoes a rapid
conversion to Nazarín's gospel which in its spontaneity and
commitment is a clear echo of the conversion of the Good Thief on
Good Friday (*10*, p.90). And yet, in a novel where several narrative
strategies have emphasized the danger of interpreting a text and its
words with absolute certainty, the defiant defence of Nazarín by *El
Sacrílego* and his claim, which will brook no opposition, that the
priest is a saint, sound dangerously extreme: 'aquí estoy yo para
responder a todo el que lo ponga en duda. A ver, pillería, ¿hay
alguien que me niegue lo que digo? Que salga el que lo niegue, y si
salen todos a la vez, aquí estoy' (V, ii; 190). However, when he
confesses privately to Nazarín his fervent desire to lead a new life
and his fears that the example of fellow criminals (including his
mother who is in Alcalá prison for infanticide) might subvert these
good intentions, his language is purged of all vulgarities and threats,
and now shines with apparent honesty, humility and, significantly,
doubt. Nazarín's final feverish vision of his new acolyte fighting the
enemy host as a 'mancebo militar y divino' (V, vi; 207) is an
idealization of the man's normal figure, 'enjuto de carnes, fisonomía
melancólica, ceja corrida y barbas ralas, la mirada en el suelo, el
paso decidido' (V, iv; 198). The truth of the matter, surely, is that the
future conduct of the reformed *El Sacrílego* cannot be firmly
predicted on the basis of this sudden conversion, although the initial
signs of a new spiritual life are promising. A definitive judgement is
simply not possible within the confines of this novel, if at all.

Even so, *El Sacrílego* emerges as a far better character than the
other prisoners in the chain gang or the host of relatives that fill the
apparently outlandish anecdotes recounted by the old beggar to
Nazarín as they walk to Madrid. The priest, bored by all this story-
telling, as usual, might, however, have listened with profit to the

moral indicated by the old raconteur, namely that he should abandon
the company of his two female followers. The old man's tag, 'no
exagero', might indeed be interpreted correctly at face value.

Fittingly, for they are the characters charged with returning the
delinquent priest and his followers to the order of Spanish society,
the two *bona fide* Civil Guards are also integrated into the *History*'s
(and the wider novel's) pattern of contrasting perspectives, and not
just because they had been prefigured by the two bogus Civil
Guards. One of the former, Cirilo Mondéjar, shows himself to be the
paragon of police virtue, arguing with his erstwhile neighbour in
Móstoles, Beatriz, that his duty to La Benemérita comes before that
to his family and friends. To let Nazarín and Andara escape would,
therefore, be a 'broma' or 'disparate' (IV, viii; 175) perhaps far more
serious than those seen in Part I. However, his and his colleague's
opinion of the priest undergo an important transformation during the
march back to Madrid: if they had thought at first he was a
'redomado hipócrita', they begin to have doubts 'pues la humildad de
sus respuestas, la paciencia callada con que sufría toda molestia, su
bondad, su dulzura, les encantaban, y acabaron por pensar que si don
Nazario no era santo, lo parecía' (V, i; 183). The verb 'encantaban' is
an ominous choice for it suggests that the Civil Guards have swung
almost to the other extreme in their views. By the novel's end, they
take pity on him, trying to comfort him, pertinently, with words. In
their complex formulation, these words synthesize the confusing use
of language in the novel, since, although the initial remarks
predicting Nazarín's release because of madness are clear and
intelligible, the subsequent, astounding implication that the whole of
Spanish society is mad is phrased in such a way that it is not
immediately obvious:

> — No tenga cuidado, padre, que allá le absolverán por
> loco. Los dos tercios de los procesados que pasan por
> nuestras manos, por locos escapan del castigo, si es que
> castigo merecen. Y presuponiendo que sea usted un
> santo, no por santo le han de soltar, sino por loco; que
> ahora priva mucho la razón de la sinrazón, o sea que la

> locura es quien hace a los muy sabios y a los muy
> ignorantes, a los que sobresalen por arriba y por abajo.
> (V, vii; 209)

In short, right up to the very last page of *Nazarín*, minor characters
are intervening in the story of the priest's adventures through words
and actions that reinforce the overall enigmatic nature of the work.
Many of them serve to alert attentive readers, if not Nazarín himself,
to the multifaceted perspectives of which human actions and words
are always capable.

3 *The Pre-History of* Nazarín

Nazarín marks, not so much a new stylistic direction in Galdós's writing as a development of tendencies evident in earlier novels. Descriptions of the Madrid *pueblo* and their living conditions had appeared in his most Zolaesque or Naturalist novels, from *La desheredada* (1881) to the *Torquemada* tetralogy (1889-95). In *Nazarín* this interest is extended — for the first time — to people and conditions in the countryside surrounding the capital. The agricultural occupations are not glamourized according to any literary tradition, but are briefly and accurately noted: workers pick vegetables, clean vineyards or clear watering holes. Other people are forced to travel from one place to another begging for a living and sleeping in tumbledown shacks in the fields. Even in such villages as Móstoles or Villamantilla, buildings and streets are in a dilapidated state. Economic conditions in the capital itself are apparently not good either. Galdós does not include these details for mere socio-economic colouring, but rather to provide a backdrop of reality against which to place the more important spiritual development of his characters, as he had done in the other novels of spiritual naturalism (starting with *Fortunata y Jacinta* (1886-87), where the term had been used as a chapter title).

Nazarín also continues an experiment Galdós had tried in two companion novels, *La incógnita* and *Realidad* (1889), where the second novel had tried to unravel the enigmas of the first by presenting the same story in dramatized form. Determining the truth of experiences still preoccupies Galdós in *Nazarín*, but now because he believes that the exercise is impossible, because of the medium of language.

Parker (*10*, p.83) goes so far as to refer *Nazarín* directly back to a much earlier novel, *Gloria* (1878), where Galdós had concluded by prophesying that the illegitimate son of Morton and Gloria, *el Nazarenito*, will have his story told one day. The prediction 'harás, sin duda, algo grande' (*OC*, IV, 599) is surprisingly echoed by the voice of Jesus at the end of *Nazarín*. Pertinent comparisons have also been made between *Nazarín* and its immediate predecessor, the *Torquemada* series: if the miser is the apostle of evil, the priest is that of good (*40*, p.362); if Torquemada is the common man, *Nazarín* is a select soul (*36*, p.182).

But if *Nazarín* is — logically — connected to previous novels of Galdós, it is also, and deliberately, built upon a surprising number of literary and historical sources in a bewildering pastiche, also reflected in the different narrative styles chosen (*9*, p.461). The first source is a generic one. We have already identified how Galdós drew a number of topographical details from guide books (Capmani and Madoz) and had given a certain prominence to journalism through the presence of a reporter, a series of journalistic interviews and journalistic stories (fires, robberies, arrests). The immediate cause for the inclusion of such material was probably Galdós's intense anger at the negative first-night reviews of his play, *Los condenados* (11 December 1894). He had countered the reviews with a hard-hitting prologue to the published text in which he levelled serious charges against the contemporary Press: it was not just a case of literature (especially the novel) getting such short shrift, but the Press, despite the improvement in technical conditions and writing, had foresaken its sacred function to mould public opinion; papers were read by more people but were believed even less, for 'la fiebre informativa ha llegado a ser tan intensa, que ella consume toda la savia intelectual del periodismo' (OC, VI, 704). Recalling his own apprenticeship as a journalist in the 1860s Galdós reminds his colleagues that he had tried to reach the reader's heart and intelligence in his articles. In other words, he is arguing for the restitution of mature commentary and analysis; journalism was more than mere factual reporting. He is not stating that there is such a thing as objective truth to be revealed by journalists, but rather that good journalism involves probing beyond the surface of events. In a letter of 8 January 1895 to Pereda enclosed with a copy of the play's text, Galdós reveals the seriousness of his intent in this prologue:

> En él me revuelvo contra los chicos de la prensa, con suavidad en la forma, con dureza en el fondo[...] la arrogancia de tales chicos y su inocencia ha [sic] llegado ya a tal punto, que no hay más remedio que pararles un poco los pies. Hoy empiezan a desatarse *los monos sabios* contra mí. Pero ya les ajustaré las cuentas otro día, si viniesen muy desmandados.[22]

The threat in Galdós's last sentence is realized perhaps in *Nazarín*, the 'desquite' for the 'error' of *Los condenados* (*35*), when the Press is ridiculed in various ways.

The obvious major historical-cum-literary source for *Nazarín* is the New Testament, for both in word and practice Nazarín endeavours to imitate Christ's life of suffering, to a degree higher than is warranted by his vocation as a priest.[23] Imitator and imitated become one so that Parker (*10*, p.92) can speak of Parts II-IV as an allegory of the life of Jesus the Nazarene, whilst Palley (*43*) adding the specific context of nineteenth-century Spain sees Nazarín as a Christ who has returned to Earth, as in Dostoievski's 'The Grand Inquisitor'.[24] The plethora of details taken by Galdós from the New

---

[22]Carmen Bravo-Villasante, '28 cartas de Galdós a Pereda', *CHA*, 84 (1970-71), 9-51 (p.47).

[23]Paco Navarro y Ledesma, in thanking Galdós for his gift of the novel, referred to it as 'El Evangelio'; letter of 12 July 1895 reproduced in *Cartas a Galdós*, ed. Soledad Ortega (Madrid: Revista de Occidente, 1964), p.327. Pageaux (*9*, p.456) calls the novel another Bible with God as author everywhere, but never announced.

[24]Alas, in an article, 'La novela novelesca', for *El Heraldo de Madrid* of 4 June 1891, defends the rights of religious and freethinkers alike to write modern humanized versions of Christ's life. Renan with his *Vie de Jésus Christ* had been the most conspicuous leader, but other Europeans (Didón, Eclersheim and Delff) had all recently explored with profit certain aspects of Jesus's life and teachings. Four years later Galdós with *Nazarín* was to join this band of Christologists — at least in part, it seems. Bowman (*16*, pp.59-

Testament naturally strengthens this identification of Nazarín with
Christ, yet at the same time, in accordance with the enigmatic
perspectives of the novel, they could also serve to highlight
important differences. It is to be remembered that these parallels of
detail, instantly recognizable to readers of the Gospels, are
marshalled by the chronicler and are not consciously sought after by
the fictional character. The only exception, when at the end of the
novel Nazarín half-sees a cross in a Madrid street and thinks of
dying a martyr's death, is immediately rejected. Parker (*10*, p.88)
maintains that Parts IV and V of the novel follow the stages of the
Passion of Christ: Nazarín's moonlit meditation on the battlements of
the castle becomes the Transfiguration; Beatriz's protestations of
loyalty recall those of St Peter at the Last Supper, whilst Beatriz
resting her head on Nazarín's shoulder suggests St John's similar
posture at the Last Supper. Andara's complaint of Nazarín's preference for Beatriz may echo Martha's complaint of Christ's favouritism
towards Mary Magdalene. Nazarín's arrest reproduces that of Christ
in the Garden of Gethsemane, especially when Andara strikes one of
the party, as St Peter smote Malchus. The arresting mayor could be
compared to Pontius Pilate, the prisoner's assault on Nazarín to the
Roman soldiers' scourging of Christ. *El Sacrílego*, as the Penitent
Thief, is given almost the same words of comfort ('Today thou shalt
be with me in Paradise'): "'Yo quiero estar con usted, señor." "Es
muy fácil. Piensa en lo que te digo y estarás conmigo'" (V, ii; 193).
Morón Arroyo (*8*, p.73) adds a further parallel: Belmonte is an
amalgam of Herod, of the rich man who refused to abandon his
wealth, and of Nicodemus the Pharisee. Andara and Beatriz can also
be viewed as representing St Paul and St John, respectively (also *24*,
p.172).

    Despite or because of the obviousness of these parallels,
contemporary reviewers of the novel welcomed its message of
Christian mysticism as an antidote to positivistic materialism, which
had proved such a failure (*35, 38, 41*). Gómez de Baquero (*36*,
p.176) summarized the varying manifestations of the contemporary

---

61) places *Nazarín* in the sixth of his categories of the Jesus myth in modern
fiction.

age's thirst for new spiritual horizons: Buddhism, gnosticism, pantheism, black magic had all been tried. So had *tolstoismo*, the New Testament fundamentalism mediated through Count Tolstoy's writings. Its traces in *Nazarín* were immediately discernible for the first reviewers (*35, 41*). In this century Portnoff (*44*) noted that as well as embodying Tolstoyan ideals, Nazarín also resembled the Russian novelist himself. Franz (*21*, p.52), believes that Belmonte's estate of La Coreja is modelled on Tolstoy's Yasnaya Polyana. Colin (*42*) and Parker (*10*) are the critics who have examined in greatest detail the Tolstoyan connections of *Nazarín*. Galdós had evidently read the 1885 Paris edition of *Ma religion*, for several pages of the copy in his library were marked. When Nazarín rejects civilization and the legal system as he leaves Madrid at the beginning of Part III, he is unwittingly practising two of Tolstoy's important precepts. Similarly when he counsels non-resistance to evil and violence or accepts poverty, he is following Tolstoy. However, there are some significant differences, where Nazarín seems to depart from the Tolstoy canon: a) in his acceptance of the rule of a Catholic Pope; b) in his fusion of Christianity and Church dogma; c) in his practice of Christianity anywhere; d) in his search for suffering and hardship (*42*, p.159). One particular episode, Beatriz's conversation with the Civil Guard, Cirilo Mondéjar, in Chapter 8, Part IV, is based on the anecdote of the grenadier and beggar in *Ma religion*, except that Galdós does not condemn the Civil Guard as Tolstoy does the grenadier. Given the departures from the Tolstoy canon and the unfulfillment of those ideals Nazarín does embody, it seems that Galdós used the Tolstoyan reminiscences, like those from the New Testament, as ironic reference points.

The second major and most obvious source of *Nazarín* is *Don Quijote*. A number of Galdós characters in other novels are, like Nazarín, natives of La Mancha, a fact that instantly signals the individual as an uncontrollable dreamer. Nazarín's departure from Madrid at the beginning of Part III reflects Don Quijote's first sally from his village in search of adventures. The actions of both idealists terminate when they are captured by a party sent out to bring them home. *Chanfaina's* boarding-house with its prostitutes is a

counterpart to the inn in Part I of *Don Quijote* where the knight
addresses a prostitute as a damsel. The Belmonte episode seems to
incorporate a number of Cervantine echoes: Don Quijote's encounter
with the circus lion, his stay at the house of Don Diego de Miranda,
and possibly that at the ducal palace. The resident chaplain of the
latter goads Don Quijote in conversation much as the mayor of
Méntrida/Aldea del Fresno does Nazarín in the jail interrogation.
The attribution of the novel (apart from Part I) to a chronicler like
Cide Hamete Benengeli, the metafictional discussion of Part I, and
the two female acolytes serving as a Sancho Panza to Nazarín's Don
Quijote, are other details that strengthen the parallel with Cervantes's
novel, most prevalent in Parts II and III. A number of commentators
(*10, 27, 29*), have criticized the addition of the *Don Quijote* parallels
for counteracting the serious trajectory of the New Testament
allusions. What these critics fail to realize is that there is a host of
allusions to literary sources other than the New Testament and *Don
Quijote*.

St Francis of Assisi is mentioned three times in the novel and
could well have been the prototype for Nazarín's new role. One
particular quality the Italian saint possessed was the ability to attract
those who had originally scorned him: in *Nazarín*, Andara, having
hurled strong abuse at Nazarín in Part I, at the beginning of Part II is
willing to follow him to the ends of the earth. Galdós's fellow
novelist and sometime lover, Pardo Bazán, had written a biography
of St Francis in 1882 and it is possible that Galdós is making a
passing recognition of this work. Certainly her interest in the tradition of the Holy Fool, to be found not only in the life of St Francis
but also in the contemporary Russian novel, could have directed
Galdós's attention towards *The Idiot* (1869) of Dostoievski. Prince
Myshkin, on the acknowledgement of his author, is a synthesis of
Don Quijote and Christ, whom he considered the two most perfect
and noble men in all of world history and literature.[25] For Palley (*43*)
there is no doubt that whereas Nazarín is the incarnation of an idea,

---

[25]In a letter of 1 January 1888 to his niece Sofia Alexandrovna; reproduced
in *Letters of Fyodor Michailovitch Dostoevsky to his Family and Friends*,
trans. Ethel Colburn Mayne, (London: Chatto and Windus, 1914), p.142.

Prince Myshkin is a character of flesh and blood with inner contradictions.

Alas (*34*, p.284) also noted the similarity of Andara's and Beatriz's discipleship to that allegedly practised by a noble mother and daughter with St Ignatius of Loyola when he was a young student at Alcalá university and not licensed to preach. It was wrongly charged that Ignatius had encouraged these women to visit a shrine at Jaén. It was also noted that a number of women would attend his preaching sessions, some of whom, like Beatriz, in a fit of hysteria or epilepsy would roll on the ground.[26]

Pattison also suggested a parallel with the inflexibly idealistic priest, Brand, eponymous protagonist of Ibsen's first major success in 1866.[27] Determined to suffer the most extreme personal hardship, like losing his mother, wife, and child (his motto is 'all or nothing'), the village priest finds, like Nazarín, a wily philosophical opponent in a materialistic village mayor.

Alas could also perhaps have suggested another contemporary Spanish novel as the genesis of Galdós's *Nazarín*: *La fe* (1892) by their common friend, Armando Palacio Valdés. This tale of provincial piety and sexual frustration culminates in the wrongful imprisonment of a charismatic young priest, Gil, for allegedly raping an adoring female parishioner who has staged the scene. Once in jail, Gil receives visits from a doctor and jurist who report their findings — that Gil is a criminal type — in the newspapers the following day. Gil is indifferent to all these developments because he has recovered his faith, temporarily lost after his frequent visits to the local *mayorazgo*, a gruff, sick misanthrope, who makes his extensive library of philosophical books available to the priest. In his review of *La fe* Alas had praised the novel as 'algo nuevo por completo en España' because of this intense religious struggle of faith by Gil, especially as contemporary Spain was not a religious country, but rather one 'donde toda gran idealidad se convierte en abstracción,

---

[26]See Paul Van Dyke, *Ignatius Loyola: The Founder of the Jesuits* (New York: Charles Scribner's Sons, 1926), pp.66-67.
[27]Walter T. Pattison, *Benito Pérez Galdós*, Twayne's World Authors Series, 341 (Boston: Twayne, 1975), p.132.

donde todas las grandezas espirituales se cristalizan en el hielo de fórmulas oficiales, académicas, eclesiásticas, según los casos.'[28] Could not Galdós have been challenged by the *succès de scandale* of *La fe* (a copy of which was in his library) to write his own shocking novel of an unorthodox priest who is prone to ecclesiastical rhetoric?

The final source figure for Nazarín — from contemporary history, not literature — is the celebrated Catalan priest and poet, Mosen Jacint Verdaguer, chaplain to the Marqués de Comillas. Appalled by the conditions of the poor in Barcelona, Verdaguer had used some of his master's money to help relieve their needs. He became particular friendly with a Deseada Martínez de Durán and her spiritualist daughter, Amparo. Verdaguer worked ceaselessly, praying at times all night, and would often be tricked by criminal types. In 1893 when he began suffering hallucinations and rumours spread that he had gone mad, the Bishop of Vich ordered him to be confined to a religious asylum, La Gleva, but two years later, when Galdós was writing *Nazarín* in Santander, Verdaguer escaped from the asylum to see his former master in Madrid. Despite the latter's instructions to the contrary, Verdaguer returned to Barcelona and lived with the Duráns. In an article for *La Prensa* of Buenos Aires in 1902 on the occasion of Verdaguer's death, Galdós disclosed (2) that he had first met the priest at the Barcelona Exhibition of 1888. Galdós sent him copies of *Nazarín* and *Halma* in which the Catalan had seen parallels with his own case (*11*, p.538). Galdós, accompanied by his friend, the Catalan novelist Narcís Oller, visited Verdaguer in Barcelona in 1896 at the Duráns' home. The description of this visit in the 1902 *La Prensa* article is strongly reminiscent, according to Boo (2, p.99) of the description of the narrator's and reporter's visit to *Chanfaina*'s house, in a remarkable example of confusion of reality and fiction.

The fact that so many sources can be advanced for different episodes and features of *Nazarín* is, in the first instance, proof that Galdós extended his game of perspectivism in the novel to include its possible sources. He knew perfectly well that practically all readers and critics of the novel would detect the New Testament and

[28]*Lunes de El Imparcial* (18 January 1892),1.

Don Quijote echoes. But only those of wider reading could perhaps extend their source-hunting to such works as *Brand*, or *The Life of St Ignatius of Loyola*, for example. This is not to invalidate the Christ and Don Quijote parallels, but merely to qualify them with other possibilities so that readers cannot argue that Nazarín is entirely another Jesus or Don Quijote. He is both of them — but only in part, as he is only in part a reflection of the other source figures. Galdós forces the readers to continually revise — without final resolution — their previous expectations and interpretations of this character, just as the narrator of Part I had spent whole days taking Nazarín apart and putting him together again in his mind at the end of Part I (*4*, p.119).

Some critics have felt that Nazarín lacks human depth as a character (*12*, p.198; *29*, p.194), one attributing this to the readers' probable awareness of the major literary models.[29] Yet it could be argued that this is just another example of Galdós playing with the readers' perspective: accustomed to regard any novel as a mirror presenting an illusion of life, they are not ready to accept the almost blatant acknowledgement by the author throughout his text of some of the literary models he has borne in mind as he wrote it, whatever the exact number and nature of those models may be. But this does not convert Nazarín into an agglutination of characteristics, words and deeds, culled from this or that source in some slavish fashion. Indeed Galdós is original (*35*) in his use of sources and there is no evidence that he had any difficulty in writing this novel; quite the contrary.[30] No, once more Galdós leaves us poised between certainty and doubt: we know that Nazarín has been built on other models, that his aim, words and behaviour are often derivative, but yet he

---

[29]Michael Nimetz, *Humor in Galdós: A Study of the 'Novelas contemporáneas'* (New Haven: Yale University Press, 1968), p.96.

[30]In a letter to Tolosa Latour of 24 May 1895, reproduced in Ruth Schmidt, *Cartas entre dos amigos del teatro: Manuel Tolosa Latour y Benito Pérez Galdós* (Las Palmas: Cabildo Insular de Gran Canaria, 1969), p.89, Galdós reported: 'me he metido en otra novela que me va saliendo muy bien, con una facilidad y una frescura que me tienen asombrado. Hay días de escribir 25 y aun 30 cuartillas. La tengo más de la mitad. Se llama Nazarín.'

surprises us with some genuine and sincere moments, even when engaged in the eternal repetition of Christian words and actions.

4 *The Post-History of* Nazarín: Halma *and Buñuel's Film*

Halma

Readers of *Nazarín* are encouraged (*7*, pp.95-96) by the closing sentence of the novel ('Yo sé que has de hacer mucho más') to expect that Galdós will continue the adventures of his priest in a sequel. Certainly contemporary reviewers (*35, 36, 38, 39*) and friends (*34*) expected as much. In a letter of 19 September 1895 Galdós indeed wrote to Paco Navarro y Ledesma: 'Estoy haciendo la segunda parte de *Nazarín*, que espero salga en octubre, o principios de noviembre.'[31] Tolosa Latour, in a letter to Galdós of 22 October 1895, suggests that the proposed title, *Condesa de Halma*, was too long for the second part of *Nazarín*,[32] whilst Alas (*34*, p.285) thinks *Halma* should have been an episode included in the *History of Nazarín*, as *El curioso impertinente* was in Part I of *Don Quijote*. Other scholars (*5*, p.100; *17*, p.126) have tended to see *Nazarín* and *Halma* as part of a trilogy, whose third element was *Misericordia*, written in 1897. However, even in *Halma* Galdós continues to dash expectations: it does not further the adventures of Nazarín in the way, for example, that Part II of *Don Quijote* does those of Part I, or the Acts of the Apostles those of the Gospels (*8, 10*). The centre of narrative gravity is moved from Nazarín and his disciples to the Condesa de Halma and her relationship with her cousin, Urrea, whom she eventually marries. Yet this may be another textual illusion, for whilst Nazarín never appears directly until Part IV of

---

[31]Reproduced in Carmen de Zulueta, *Navarro Ledesma, el hombre y su tiempo* (Madrid: Alfaguara, 1968), pp.292-93.
[32]Reproduced in Sebastián de la Nuez & José Schraibman, *Cartas del archivo de Pérez Galdós* (Madrid: Taurus, 1967), p.315.

Halma, he and his party are the major topic of interest and conversation throughout the first three parts. After he has been released from hospital where his illness has been diagnosed by a psychiatrist and nerve specialist as 'melancolía religiosa', a form of 'neurosis epiléptica', Nazarín is entrusted by the religious authorities to Halma. It is Nazarín who advises her to abandon the idea of a religious commune at Pedralba, return to the civilization of Madrid and settle into married life with Urrea.[33] So Nazarín's role in *Halma* is not insignificant. Furthermore, whilst he exerts strong effects on new characters like Halma and the priest, Manuel Flórez, these developments are related to the character of the priest as presented in *Nazarín*. References to his appearance in the latter and discussion of certain incidents and the chronicler's attitudes allow Galdós to answer criticisms as Cervantes did in Part II of *Don Quijote*. This fiction within a fiction provides another example of metafictional commentary that underlines the supremacy of the fictional process at work in these two novels. An examination of these passages in *Halma* is therefore justifiable in an attempt to cast light on the meaning of *Nazarín*.

Opinions on the priest are still divided into two opposing camps: he is either a saint or a fool. Attempts to resolve the enigma are led by the journalists who swarm around the innumerable visitors to Nazarín's room in the hospital. Their efforts are limited to reporting the most trivial and external details of Nazarín's daily routine. Clearly Galdós is continuing his sharp attack on the popular Press: even the impetuous reporter reappears with more strong language: Nazarín is 'un tío muy largo, pero muy largo[...] patriarca de los tumbones y[...] Mesías de la gorronería[...] hace su papel con un histrionismo perfecto' (*OC*, V, 1811).

The first number of Urrea's new review with biographical information and photographs of Nazarín and his disciples is hardly better. Like the 'tertulianos' of the Feramor household and such painters as Sorolla and Moreno Carbonero, who sketch the priest in

---

[33]Pedralbes was the name of a country estate owned by the Marqués de Comillas to which his widowed aunt moved once Verdaguer started using the family mansion in Barcelona for séances (*11*, p.539).

hospital, Urrea shows an obsessive interest in the external physical features that only extends — pointlessly — the list of analogues suggested in my previous chapter: 'fíjense, fíjense bien en la cara de Nazarín. ¿Es Job, es Mahoma, es San Francisco, es Abelardo, es Pedro el Ermitaño, es Isaías, es el propio Sem, hijo de Noé? ¡Enigma inmenso!' (*OC*, V, 1793).

To the questions of Feramor ('Pero ese Nazarín, ¿qué es?', *OC*, V, 1792) and of Halma ('¿quién es Nazarín?', *OC*, V, 1796), Manuel Flórez at first responds with background information about his previous acquaintance with the priest in the church of San Cayetano (not reported in *Nazarín*). Increasingly, though, Flórez's reactions are of confusion and bewilderment, after initially believing — naively — like the reporter in Part I of *Nazarín*, that he will 'llegar a la certidumbre con sólo tratarle un poco, analizar sus ideas y someter a un examen prolijo sus acciones' (*OC*, V, 1801). Flórez cannot get Nazarín's inner character in focus, just as the bodies of *Chanfaina* and Ujo were an optical confusion for observers in *Nazarín*: 'la persona del asendereado clérigo se iba creciendo a sus ojos, y al fin en tales proporciones le veía, que no acertaba a formular un juicio terminante' (*OC*, V, 1809). Flórez's conclusion, which will drive him to madness and to death, is really that the enigma is unsolvable and has to be accepted as such.

Halma at first has more confidence in deciphering the enigma, now somewhat more qualified ('¿Es un loco santo o un santo loco?', *OC*, V, 1817); 'Y mis dudas[...] van a ser el punto de partida para resolver la cuestión, porque si no dudáramos, no nos propondríamos, como nos proponemos ahora, llegar a la verdad' (*OC*, V, 1817). Flórez's mechanically-articulated agreement hints at an underlying scepticism: Halma will probably be forced to accept the paradox, as she then foresees: ' Y si existieran juntas y confundidas en una misma planta[...] respetaríamos este fenómeno incomprensible, y nos quedaríamos tristes y desconsolados, pero con nuestra conciencia tranquila' (*OC*, V, 1818). Through both Flórez and Halma Galdós is assuredly repeating the lesson of his previous novel: the inadvisability and impossibility of trying to reach definitive, unidimensional judgements, whether after direct experience of reality (here Flórez's visits to Nazarín) or after the mediation of literature, for Halma's experience of Nazarín is through what she has read of the novel *Nazarín*, supplemented naturally by Flórez's first-hand observations.

Galdós surpasses his model Cervantes in the confusion of the fictional and real worlds when the narrator records that Halma's copy of *Nazarín* was a gift of 'su autor, con una dedicatoria muy expresiva' (*OC*, V, 1797). Halma's comments on what she has read permit Galdós to again reinforce — through her errors of interpretation — the thrust of his message in *Nazarín*. Halma declares: 'Pero no me fío de lo que allí se cuenta, por ser obra más bien imaginativa que histórica. Los escritores del día, antes procuran deleitar con la fantasía que instruir con la verdad' (*OC*, V, 1797). For his part, Flórez is persuaded to study Nazarín in the flesh, for 'El sujeto vivo dará más luz que una historia cualquiera, aun suponiendo que no fuese fantástica y tan sólo escrita para entretenimiento de los desocupados' (*OC*, V, 1797). Both characters are mistaken in these beliefs. If Halma had read *Nazarín* carefully enough, she would have recalled the confusing disquisition of the narrator of Part I on whether Parts II-V were a novel or a history. Flórez will soon realize that his live study of the priest will prove just as perplexing and inconclusive as any number of readings of the text entitled *Nazarín*.

Nazarín's reactions to the fictionalization of his adventures, reported at second hand, also stress fiction's distortion of the truth: 'el autor movido de su afán de novelar los hechos, le enaltece demasiado, encomiando con exceso acciones comunes que no pertenecen al orden del heroísmo, ni aun al de la virtud extraordinaria' (*OC*, V, 1812). Nazarín rejects his status as a hero in the campaign of Villamanta, for he is not 'un personaje poemático o novelesco', a belief that does not square with his proven status in the novel, *Nazarín*. Like all readers, perhaps, the priest would prefer a less confusing and less multidimensional interpretation of the text. Fallible as any reader, he is made to commit the error of confusing the identity of the prison (Navalcarnero, not Móstoles) where he had difficulty — now, apparently, not too much — in conquering his anger after *El Parricida*'s attack (*OC*, V, 1812).[34]

Andara also continues the process of rectification for, as she declares to the 'chicos de la Prensa', *Nazarín* is full of lies and the '*escribiente*[...] es un embustero' (*OC*, V, 1813): the fire at *Chanfaina*'s was an accident, a line of defence suggested by her lawyer that will later acquit her of the charge of arson and reduce her final prison sentence (*OC*, V, 1817). In one final touch of mock literary self-flagellation Galdós has Andara upbraid him for painting her as an ugly woman: 'Es que me encalabrino cuando me hablan del maldito libraco. ¡Miren que decir ese *desgalichao* autor que yo parezco un palo vestido! Fea soy[...] pero no tan fea que me tenga miedo la gente. El será un esperpento, y en sus escrituras quiere hacer conmigo una *desageración* ¿Verdad que no tanto?' (*OC*, V, 1813).

The review of *Nazarín* by its protagonist enables Galdós to advance indirectly a defence against the charges of following Russian models in his picture of Nazarín's mystical evangelism, or in other words, the novel's 'tolstoismo'. Flórez, who is charged with the rebuttal, argues at length to the 'chicos de la Prensa' that, as Spain is the land of mysticism and knight-errantry, Nazarín's ideas are not exceptional importations from Russia. Nazarín himself is reported to have said that he knows nothing of Russian literature and that since human feelings and ideas know no frontiers, it is 'naturalísimo que en Oriente y Occidente haya almas que sientan lo mismo, y plumas que escriban cosas semejantes' (*OC*, V, 1811). In highlighting just one of his probable sources, albeit for the immediate purpose of defence against charges of plagiarism, Galdós also succeeds in continuing the perspectives of confusion created by *Nazarín*: the naive reader of *Halma* could be forgiven for believing that 'tolstoismo' was the only source for the former.

When Nazarín does appear directly in *Halma*, at the house of the country priest, Don Remigio, the external changes are most striking: now dressed in a priest's cassock and cleanly shaven, he is

---

[34]An aristocrat amongst the hospital visitors, who is a cousin of Belmonte, rejects the episode at La Coreja as pure fiction (*OC*, V, 1812).

occupied — irony of ironies — in making a précis of a book of sermons on the virtue of patience. He can also laugh slightly at his previous madness when rejecting Urrea's request to be admitted as a 'loco' to Pedralba: ' — ¡Oh, no! Para locos, bastante tienen conmigo — replicó don Nazario, con inflexión humorística, casi casi perceptible' (*OC*, V, 1848). Nazarín's advisory function is represented as telling the truth, a process to which he was much given in *Nazarín*: 'Si usted no ha visto aún esa verdad, conviene que yo se la ponga delante de los ojos' (*OC*, V, 1866); 'Nada soy, y si alguna vez no fuera órgano de la verdad, de poco valdría mi existencia' (*OC*, V, 1869); 'No soy la primera inteligencia del mundo; pero Dios quiere que en esta ocasión pueda yo manifestar verdades que avasallen y cautiven su gran entendimiento, permitiéndole realizar los fines que se propone' (*OC*, V, 1868). For *Halma*, Nazarín is indeed 'el misionero de la verdad, el emisario del Verbo Divino' (*OC*, V, 1870); and we recall Ujo's determination to fight the latter, in order to defend Andara. But there are important differences between Nazarín's concepts of truth in the two novels: in *Halma* he no longer states that it is an objective truth, but rather that it is qualified because of his subjective perspective: 'la verdad, tal como en mí la siento' (*OC*, V, 1866). This is no longer the truth of Christian dogma, but the human truth about the two individuals for whose mutual benefit it is related. And yet Galdós, as he was wont to do in *Nazarín*, undercuts our acceptance of this reformed vision of truth by stating in the last chapter of *Halma* that all of the material in the present novel has been scrupulously reproduced from documents in the 'archivo nazarista' (*OC*, V, 1872), the same suspect and contradictory source for Parts II-V of *Nazarín*. *Halma* does indeed continue the methodological reading lesson of its predecessor.

Buñuel's Film of Nazarín

The merit of studying Buñuel's 1959 black-and-white film (95 minutes) lies not so much in the place this film occupies in the director's work as in the perceptive reading it offers of Galdós's novel, like his subsequent version of another Galdós novel, *Tristana*.

Whilst there are surprising reproductions of Galdós's words, especially at the strangest of places, for example in Andara's conversations with Nazarín in Part II (*47*, p.139), there are, of course, more substantive changes, perhaps designed to upset, like the novel itself, our expectations of what should appear on the screen. Certainly Christian values are no longer to the fore, and Buñuel instead stresses the uselessness of religion, its masochism and repression of sexual instincts (*45, 48*). The setting is moved to the Mexico of Porfirio Díaz in 1900. All three major interviews with Nazarín seem to have been omitted, with the reporter of Part I being replaced by an engineer installing electric lighting in *Chanfaina*'s inn, where half of the film takes place, but not at Carnaval time. Nazarín's distant encounter in Part III with soldiers on manoeuvres is replaced in the film by a scene with railway navvies. The castle scene at Méntrida/Aldea del Fresno has been transformed into a stable scene. The emphasis in the film version falls on the relations of Nazarín with his two disciples and theirs with their respective male admirers. In Buñuel's film, Pinto does succeed in returning Beatriz to her home: his carriage triumphantly passes the chain gang on the road, unnoticed by the priest gazing at the ground before him. The film closes soon after this shot when Nazarín changes his mind and accepts the offer of a pineapple from a roadside vendor. It has been argued (*55*) that this final sequence confirms Nazarín's progress during the film, from the illusions offered by religion to the discovery of Man's essential need of his fellow human beings. It could also be argued that this transition is too sudden and unprepared, that the film's ending, like Galdós's novel, presents the audience with a picture of a character whose basically enigmatic nature is never satisfactorily elucidated.

5 *Conclusion*

The chapters of this study have been arranged in an order that might correspond to the general reader's approach: reading the text first and then expanding the interpretative focus to explore related matters like sources and sequels. The numbering and length of the respective chapters and their divisions represent a break with traditional and expected formats so as to better capture the shifting perspectives of the text itself and the impossibility of getting people, objects, words, actions, sources, or influences into a single, fixed perspective of interpretation. Readers are constantly shown by precept and example the dangers of seeking an objective truth when individual subjectivity controls any assessment of the text and its components - Urey (*32*, p.59) is perhaps over-optimistic in believing that irony can point the reader towards this hidden ultimate truth. Readers are obliged to accept the contradictions and uncertainties of the text, recognizing that Nazarín can be considered a saint for his attempt to preach and practise the Gospel of Christ, or a fool for attempting to do this in a literal fashion that ignores the reality of nineteenth-century Spanish society, or both, in varying degrees. Uncertainty extends, perforce, to the development of the three principal characters (how far do they really change through their interaction?) and even to the respective importance of vastly different components in a sentence or chapter — for example in Part I the discussion of a street name seems to count for as much as the presentation of the novel's eponymous hero. And, of course, it does, in relative terms, for the former is an important mini-lesson on confusing designations that will well apply to Nazarín. The relativity of the subjective experience permeates any interpretation of the text of the novel. Nonetheless, readers are forced to accept the text as it stands; they cannot arbitrarily change the words, only their plurivalent meaning, according to the perspective adapted for each reading of the text.

Some critics have maintained that *Nazarín* is not one of Galdós's best novels: Palley (*43*) maintains that 'los matices, la sutileza y la profundidad de su mejor obra' are not present in *Nazarín*, whilst Ruiz Ramón (*29*, p.194), in a pithy phrase, reckons that 'Galdós no ha creado una gran novela, pero nos ha dejado un personaje inolvidable'. On the contrary, Nazarín is perhaps a forgettable character as he doggedly tries to live his new life according to a preconceived plan — Ujo is far more memorable —, and *Nazarín* is a great novel, whose well-crafted text is a constant challenge to the readers to question or reassess their interpretation of the text and, by extension, of related, loftier texts. Cavia (*35*) was certainly correct when he prophesied, 'De *Nazarín* ha de hablarse y escribirse mucho', but guilty of the same fault as Nazarín, other characters of the novel and its readers, when he hoped that there would be no disagreement with his praise of the novel: 'y yo espero en el Dios de aquel varón justo y de los pobres humildes y desheredados que le siguieron por "tierra de Madrid" que por esta vez la crítica ha de aclamar a Galdós, sin que nadie discrepe y se alce contra nuestro *hosana*.' Conflicting readings of the novel and contradictory assessments of its meaning are the inevitable consequence of the narrative mode employed. Any study — and this one is no exception — must take its place in this pattern, liable to subsequent and continuous confirmation, rectification, and rejection.

Bibliographical Note

A. Bibliographies

For details of the editions of *Nazarín* see Miguel Hernández Suárez, *Bibliografía de Galdós*, vol. I (Las Palmas: Cabildo Insular, 1972), pp.147-50. There is no English translation of the novel.

For further critical studies see: Theodore A. Sackett, *Pérez Galdós: An Annotated Bibliography* (Albuquerque: University of New Mexico Press, 1968); Hensley C. Woodbridge, *Benito Pérez Galdós: A Selective Annotated Bibliography* (Metuchen, NJ: Scarecrow Press, 1975); *Benito Pérez Galdós: An Annotated Bibliography for 1975-1980* (Watertown, MA: General Microfilm, 1981); J. E. Varey, 'Galdós in the Light of Recent Criticism', in *Galdós Studies*, ed. Varey (London: Tamesis, 1970), pp.1-35; Luciano García Lorenzo, 'Bibliografía galdosiana', *CHA*, 84 (1970-71), 758-97; Miguel Hernández Suárez, 'Bibliografía', *AG*, 3 (1968), 191-212; 4 (1969), 127-52; 6 (1971), 139-63; 7 (1972), 145-65; 9 (1974), 175-206.

B. Articles on *'Nazarín'*

1. P.A. Bly, *'Nazarín*: ¿enigma eterno o triunfo del arte galdosiano?', *CHA*, 124 (1981), 286-300. The contradictions in Nazarín's character.
2. Matilde L. Boo, 'Una nota acerca de Verdaguer y Nazarín', *AG*, 13 (1978), 99-100. A corroborative sequel to *10*.
3. Francisco Carenas, 'Nazarín: una rebelión eclesial', *Papeles de Son Armadans*, 75 (1974), 107-20. Uncritical acceptance of Nazarín's itinerant evangelism.
3a. Francisco Carenas, 'La desalienación esquemocrática en *Nazarín', Iris* (1990), 15-24. An optimistic view of Nazarín's abandonment of the cassock for the cape when he leaves Madrid: both in word and deed the true Christian replaces the professional priest.
4. Brian J. Dendle, 'Point of View in *Nazarín*: An Appendix to Goldman', *AG*, 9 (1974), 113-21. Excellent study of the chronicler of Parts II-V, and of Nazarín's egotism.

4a. Stacey L. Dolgin, '*Nazarín*: a Tribute to Galdós' Indebtedness to Cervantes', *Hispanófila*, no. 97 (Sep. 1989), 17-22. A brief, general, arguable review of the essential role played by the ironic multiple viewpoints of *Don Quijote* in the establishment of the Christ-Nazarín parallel.

5. Peter B. Goldman, 'Galdós and the Aesthetic of Ambiguity: Notes on the Thematic Structure of *Nazarín*', *AG*, 9 (1974), 99-112. An excellent examination of the ambiguities of Part I and the Belmonte episode.

6. Agnes Gullón, 'Escenario, personaje y espacio en *Nazarín*', in *Actas del Segundo Congreso Internacional de Estudios Galdosianos*, II (Las Palmas: Cabildo Insular de Gran Canaria, 1980), pp.211-22. A cogent demonstration of how the transition from urban to rural scenery at the end of Part II produces a mental/spiritual space.

6a. Brigitte Journeau, 'Nazarín, dissonances et consonances avec l'esprit d'un temps,' *Minorités et marginalités en Espagne et en Amérique Latine* (Lille: Presses Universitaires de Lille, 1990), pp.47-59. An interesting, though debatable and slightly meandering, examination of Nazarín as Galdós's individual incarnation of a truly Christian spirit.

7. John W. Kronik, 'Estructuras dinámicas en *Nazarín*', *AG*, 9 (1974), 81-98. A very detailed account of Nazarín's spiritual progress through the novel as represented by his physical movements. Some excellent remarks on Nazarín's status as a literary myth.

7a. Mariano López, 'Antinaturalismo y humanismo en Galdós: *Angel Guerra, Nazarín y Halma*', *Hispania*, 61 (1978), 69-77. Galdós's starting-point is a Christian, spiritualist view of life.

8. Ciriaco Morón Arroyo, '*Nazarín y Halma*: sentido y unidad', *AG*, 2 (1967), 67-81. Misleadingly-entitled study, disjointed and rambling, with the occasional point of interest, as, for instance, the similarities of *Nazarín* to Renan's *La Vie de Jésus*.

9. Daniel-Henri Pageaux, 'Eléments pour une lecture de *Nazarín*', *Revue de Littérature Comparée*, 58 (1978), 455-65. Accurate observations on the parallels with the *Divina commedia*, Nazarín's search for spiritual rebirth in the countryside, and the pastiche of literary styles Galdós uses.

10. Alexander A. Parker, '*Nazarín*, or the Passion of Our Lord Jesus Christ According to Ga'dós', *AG*, 2 (1967), 83-101. A brilliantly-argued interpretation of the novel as an allegory.

11. Walter T. Pattison, 'Verdaguer y Nazarín', *CHA*, 84 (1970-71), 537-45. Good detective work on the similarities between a possible real-life model and his fictional counterpart.

12. Alberto Rábago, 'Nazarín: su evolución como personaje novelesco',*Explicación de Textos Literarios*, 5 (1976), 197-205. Diminishes Nazarín's weaknesses by championing him as a true imitator of Christ.

12a Claire-Nicolle Robin, 'Nazarín o el problema de la libertad individual
    en 1895', in *Actas del tercer congreso internacional de estudios
    galdosianos* II (Las Palmas: Cabildo Insular de Gran Canaria, 1990),
    pp.159-69. Interesting presentation of Nazarín as the representative of
    an anachronistic system of values at odds with those of modern urban
    society, in which individual liberty is the fundamental problem.

13. Francisco Romero Pérez, 'Nazarín: Galdós' Enigmatic Apostle', *Revista
    de Estudios Hispánicos* (Alabama), 17 (1983), 189-98. Somewhat
    repetitive in emphasizing the transformation of Nazarín from self-
    centered recluse in *Nazarín* to self-knowing social conformist at the
    end of *Halma*.

14. J. Sinnigen, 'The Search for a New Totality in *Nazarín, Halma,
    Misericordia*', *Modern Language Notes*, 93 (1978), 233-51. Criticizes
    Nazarín's egotism as a factor in his failure to transcend contemporary
    bourgeois society.

15. Hadassah Ruth Weiner, 'A Note on *Nazarín*', *AG*, 13 (1978), 101-03.
    The Old Testament connotations of Nazarín's name.

C. Sections on 'Nazarín' in General Studies

16. Frank P. Bowman, 'On the Definition of Jesus in Modern Fiction', *AG*,
    2 (1967), 53-66. A fascinating review of *Nazarín*'s position within the
    various categories of narratives on the Jesus figure, 1780-1940.

17. Joaquín Casalduero, *Vida y obra de Benito Pérez Galdós (1843-1920)*,
    3rd ed. (Madrid: Gredos, 1970), pp.124-27. Pioneering study of
    Nazarín's spiritualism.

18. Gustavo Correa, 'Tradición mística y cervantismo en las novelas de
    Galdós, 1890-97', *Hispania* (U.S.A.), 53 (1970), 842-51. The odd
    observation of interest in this review of *Nazarín* and the other
    spiritualist novels.

19. ——, *El simbolismo religioso en las novelas de Pérez Galdós* (Madrid:
    Gredos, 1962), pp.166-79. Uncritical, descriptive account of Nazarín's
    rise to supernatural, spiritual status.

20. Sherman H. Eoff, *The Novels of Pérez Galdós: The Concept of Life as
    Dynamic Process* (St Louis: Washington University, 1954), pp.69-72.
    Somewhat schematized analysis.

21. Thomas R. Franz, *Remaking Reality in Galdós: A Writer's Interactions
    with his Context* (Athens, OH: Strathmore Press, 1982), pp.26-53.
    Ingenious piece of detective work, identifying character traits of
    Rousseau in Nazarín, and of Tolstoy in Belmonte.

22. Ricardo Gullón, *Galdós, novelista moderno* (Madrid: Taurus, 1960),
    pp.108-09. Brief, incisive appraisal.

23. Georges Haldas, *Trois écrivains de la relation fondamentale: Pérez Galdós, Giovanni Verga, C. F. Ramuz* (Lausanne: L'Age d'Homme, 1978), pp.25-59. A jerky account of Nazarín's (Galdós's) search for God in other humans.

24. José Luis Mora García, *Hombre, sociedad y religión en la novelística galdosiana (1884-1905)* (Salamanca: Universidad de Salamanca and Cabildo Insular de Gran Canaria, 1981), pp.163-81. The occasional insight.

25. Daniel-Henri Pageaux, 'Sur quelques "retours à la nature" dans la littérature espagnole fin de siècle', *Romantisme*, 30 (1980), 49-59. Intelligent comparisons of *Nazarín* with *Peñas arriba* by Pereda and *En torno al casticismo* by Unamuno, all published in the same year.

26. Gilberto Paolini, *An Aspect of Spiritualistic Naturalism in the Novels of Benito Pérez Galdós: Charity* (New York: Las Américas, 1969), pp.91-102. Unearths examples of this theme.

26a. Arnold M. Penuel, *Psychology, Religion and Ethics in Galdós's Novels. The Quest for Authenticity.* (Lanham, Maryland: 1987), pp.111-20. A debatable optimistic view of Nazarín's 'quest for authenticity'.

27. Francisco Pérez Gutiérrez, *El problema religioso en la generación de 1868* (Madrid: Taurus, 1975), pp.250-52. Too encyclopedic.

28. Robert Ricard, 'La "segunda conversión" en las novelas de Galdós', *Revista de Occidente*, new series 4 (1964), 114-18. The attainment of true Christian perfection by Nazarín.

29. Francisco Ruiz Ramón, *Tres personajes galdosianos: ensayo de aproximación a un mundo religioso y moral* (Madrid: Revista de Occidente, 1964), pp.174-95. Lucid exposition of Nazarín's practical sanctity and the Christ and Don Quixote parallels, albeit with some debatable conclusions.

30. Stephen Scatori, *La idea religiosa en la obra de Benito Pérez Galdós* (Toulouse: Edouard Privat, 1927), pp.79-85. Reasonable, but brief, observations.

31. Guillermo de Torre, 'Nueva estimativa de las novelas de Galdós', *Cursos y Conferencias*, 24 (October 1943-March 1944), 25-37. Some perceptive remarks from time to time.

32. Diane F. Urey, *Galdós and the Irony of Language* (Cambridge: University Press, 1982), pp.55-59, 66-67. A brilliant, very detailed analysis of the working of irony in the first chapter of *Nazarín*.

33. Theodore Ziolkowski, *Fictional Transfigurations of Jesus* (Princeton: University Press, 1972), pp.68-78. With greater textual references than Bowman (*16*), inserts *Nazarín* into the corpus of nineteenth-century fictionalized, Christian socialist tracts.

D *Contemporary Reviews*

34. Leopoldo Alas, *Galdós* (Madrid: Renacimiento, 1912), pp.277-81.
     Points out the picaresque tone of the novel.
35. Mariano de Cavia, 'Letras de molde: *Nazarín', El Heraldo de Madrid*
     (15 July 1895), 1. Suggests the influence of Tolstoy.
36. E. Gómez de Baquero, 'El problema religioso en dos novelas:
     Torquemada y San Pedro y Nazarín', EM (August 1895), 174-87. Has
     high praise for *Nazarín's* reflection of the intellectual yearnings of the
     time.
37. ——, '*Halma, Nazarín* y el misticismo ruso', *EM* (January 1896), 147-
     53. Accurate assessment of the relationship of the two novels.
38. Norberto González Aurioles, '*Nazarín*, novela por D. Benito Pérez
     Galdós', *El Correo* (25 July 1895), 1. Perceptive, with enthusiastic
     approval of Galdós's solution of evangelism for contemporary society.
39. Kasabal, *La Ilustración Ibérica* (27 July 1895), 467. A positive review.
40. H. Peseux-Richard, *Revue Hispanique*, 3 (1896), 362-63. Critical of the
     undeveloped *Quijote* associations.
41. Zeda, '*Nazarín', La Epoca* (16 July 1895), 1. Notes echoes of Tolstoy,
     with approval of the novel's Christian message.

E. '*Nazarín' and the Russian Novel*

42. Vera Colin, 'A Note on Tolstoy and Galdós', *AG*, 2 (1967), 155-68.
     Pioneer work on the influence of *Ma religion* on *Nazarín*, with an
     occasional tendency to overstate Galdós's attitude.
43. Julián Palley, '*Nazarín y El idiota', In*, no.258 (May 1968), 3.
     Compares the debt of both Galdós and Dostoievski to Cervantes, rating
     Myshkin above Nazarín.
44. George Portnoff, *La literatura rusa en España* (New York: Instituto de
     las Españas, 1932), pp.173-205. Not so detailed a study of Tolstoy's
     influence as *42*.

F. *Galdós and Buñuel*

45. Max Aub, 'Galdós et *Nazarín', Les Lettres Françaises*, no.151
     (December 1960), 7. Brief generalities.
46. Freddy Buache. *Luis Buñuel* (Lausanne: L'Age d'Homme, 1970),
     pp.89-97. Indicates the general change of direction Buñuel gave to
     Galdós's story.
47. Luis Buñuel, *The Exterminating Angel, Nazarín and Los Olvidados:
     Three Films by Luis Buñuel*, translated by Nicholas Fry (London:
     Lorrimer Publishing, 1972), pp.105-205. The English translation of the
     filmscript with stills. Also included are those dialogues that in the film
     version were omitted from the original scenario.

48. Fernando C. Cesarman, *El ojo de Buñuel: psicoanálisis desde una butaca* (Barcelona: Anagrama, 1976), pp.143-59. A useful synopsis of the film's plot. Emphasizes the repressed sexuality of Buñuel's three main characters.

49. Jean Domarchi, '*Nazarín*, de Buñuel ou Eros contre le Christ', *Arts*, no.799 (7 December 1960), 7. Believes that Buñuel attacks religion with the weapon of eroticism.

50. Michel Estève, '*Nazarín* et *Le Journal d'un curé de campagne*: la passion refusée et acceptée', *Etudes Cinématographiques*, 10-11 (1961), 217-34. Alludes to some differences between the novel and the film version.

51. Gérard Gozlan, 'Les Lettres du générique sont en forme de croix (Nazarín)', *Positif*, no.42 (November 1961), 31-51. Detailed analysis of the film with some debatable interpretations of the novel.

52. Gavin Lambert, '*Nazarín*', *Film Quarterly*, 13, no. 3 (1960), 30-31. Enthusiastic but incorrect information on Galdós.

52a. Gastón Lillo, 'De *Nazarín* de Galdós a Nazarín de Buñuel. La adaptación cinematográfica como "lectura crítica"', *Lenguas, Literaturas, Sociedades*, 2 (1989), 115-26. Failing to see the irony at work in *Nazarín*, he overstates the case for regarding the film as a subversion of the novel.

53. Octavio Paz, '*Nazarín*', *Film Culture*, 21 (1960), 60-62. Measured and perceptive views of both the film and the novel.

54. Manuel Rabanal Taylor, '*Nazarín*: Galdós visto por Buñuel', *In*, no.163 (June 1960), 14. Highlights the changes which Buñuel introduced into Galdós's story.

55. Georges Sadoul, 'Un nouveau Don Quichotte', *Les Lettres Françaises* (8 December 1960), 10. Nazarín's chief discovery is his religious doubt.

CRITICAL GUIDES TO SPANISH TEXTS

Edited by
J.E. Varey, A.D. Deyermond & S.M. Hart